T0163347

The Question of MacArthur's Reputation

★

The Question of

MacArthur's

Reputation

★ ★

CÔTE DE CHÂTILLON, OCTOBER 14–16, 1918

Robert H. Ferrell

UNIVERSITY OF MISSOURI PRESS
COLUMBIA AND LONDON

Library of Congress Cataloging-in-Publication Data

Ferrell, Robert H.
    The question of MacArthur's reputation : Côte de Châtillon, October 14–16,
1918 / Robert H. Ferrell.
        p.   cm.
Includes bibliographical references and index.
Summary: "Ferrell examines the WWI battle at Côte de Châtillon, reconstructing the
movements of troops and the decisions of officers to detail how MacArthur's
subordinates were the true heroes and how the taking of the hill could have been a
disaster had the Eighty-fourth Brigade followed the general's original plan"
—Provided by publisher.
    ISBN 978-0-8262-1830-8 (alk. paper)
    1. Côte de Châtillon, Battle of, France, 1918.   2. MacArthur, Douglas, 1880–1964—
Military leadership.   3. United States. Army. Infantry Regiment, 167th.   4. World War,
1914–1918—Regimental histories—United States.   I. Title.
    D545.A63F48 2008
    940.4'36—dc22

                                                                                    2008026294

∞ This paper meets the requirements of the American National Standard for
Permanence of Paper for Printed Library Materials, Z39.48, 1984.

Designer: Kristie Lee
Typesetter: BookComp, Inc.
Printer and binder: Thomson-Shore, Inc.
Typefaces: Minion, Fashion Compressed

Contents

★ ★

Preface

★ ★

General Douglas MacArthur was not one to hide his light. He told a fellow officer, Major General Charles D. Rhodes, that there were two kinds of generals, one merely administrators, the other leaders of men in the field. At the côte, or hill, of Châtillon, he said, on October 14–16, 1918, he led the troops, inspiring them by example.[1]

General MacArthur gained his military reputation in the taking of Châtillon during the great battle of the Meuse-Argonne in World War I, in which he commanded the Eighty-fourth Infantry Brigade of the Forty-second Division. His troops, the 167th Infantry Regiment, drawn from members of the Alabama National Guard, and the 168th Infantry, from the Iowa Guard, together with allotted portions of the division's artillery brigade and the machine gun regiment, took the hill and broke the main German line in northern France. But the question is twofold: what happened at Châtillon, and what did MacArthur have to do with it? On these scores the record has not been clear. In writing about the Meuse-Argonne, I have been struck by the inexactness of the accounts of Châtillon.[2] The regimental histories describe the regiments. The divisional history is a hopeless muddle of 888 pages, without an index, written by a general, everything defined repetitively, full of quotations, many of them eyewitness stories but muddled by the general.[3] Biographies of MacArthur assert his leadership at Châtillon but do not describe it. The three-volume biography by D. Clayton James (who once told me, when I commiserated with him on his subject, that he "spent fifteen years with the s.o.b.") does not do much with Châtillon—a few pages from easily available sources; no use of U.S. Army records now deposited in a huge building in College Park, Maryland; no personal records from the Military History Institute, a part of the Army War College in Carlisle Barracks, near Harrisburg, Pennsylvania.[4]

The pages that follow look closely into Châtillon, to determine if what MacArthur told General Rhodes was true. For the reputations of military men, political leaders, and, for that matter, financial leaders—I write in the year 2008, when the subprime mortgage problem has brought the dismissals of major figures in Wall Street—are so fragile, almost evanescent. The passage of time changes so much of our understanding. Opinion dominates until, over the years, information narrows the guesswork, makes the unclear less difficult to decipher. One might even say that military leadership is more difficult to be sure of than the simpler dimensions of politics and economics. Military leaders function in what the Prussian military thinker Karl von Clausewitz described as the fog of war, frequently making decisions amid great confusion. But the elapse of years, decades now since the death of General MacArthur in 1964, makes measurement easier, and in that respect it is time for the examination of the general's reputation.

Acknowledgments

★ ★

No book can be written without help, and for this one I am indebted to three research librarians at Indiana University in Bloomington, David K. Frasier, Jeffrey C. Graf, and Louise Malcomb; in the complexity of present-day libraries it is simply necessary to have such assistance, and I knew from the outset how competent it would be, having relied upon them before. Andrew J. Dunar and J. Garry Clifford sought out manuscript sources, for which I am very grateful. Mitchell Yockelson and Timothy Nenninger of the National Archives again gave help, as only skilled archivists can do. Similarly, over the years, I have been aided by the archivist at the U.S. Army Military History Institute in Carlisle Barracks, David A. Keough. The General Harold Keith Johnson Professor of Military History at the Army War College, Richard J. Sommers, was far more helpful than anything I could have expected, even though he is an old friend. He not merely informed me in detail about the disorganized nature of General Henry J. Reilly's papers but also gave specific advice on how to get at what was there—in a collection of 130 boxes. He kindly searched through the organized boxes, one-third of the collection. My friend John Slonaker, a longtime scholar of the Institute, searched the others. Lori Miller searched the personnel records of General Douglas MacArthur at the federal records center in St. Louis. I am especially grateful to Martha Braley, the granddaughter of Major Lloyd D. Ross, for allowing me to see his voluminous diary and other of her grandfather's papers; my thanks, too, to Martha Braley's daughter, Lynn Miller, for sending the papers.

I am much in debt to the director of the University of Missouri Press, Beverly Jarrett, for enthusiasm, which she always has, and advice on how to organize the manuscript. As always, it is a pleasure to work with her, for all manuscripts have uncertainties, especially in their beginnings. The managing editor of the press, Jane Lago, similarly makes everything easier because of her clearheaded sense of what is understandable (obtained, I like to think, in part at Indiana University, where I taught for many years and where she studied some years ago). Martin Northway, also formerly of Bloomington, Indiana, provided astute proofreading. Betty J. Bradbury was the excellent word processor; John M. Hollingsworth, the cartographer. Of course both of them are residents of Bloomington.

Carolyn, Lorin, and Amanda helped in many ways.

Let me add a sense of awkwardness to my narrative and its conclusions, because of a very pleasant cooperation with the officers and the singularly helpful archivist, James W. Zobel, of the MacArthur Foundation in Norfolk, Virginia, some years ago, when I sought to bring together another manuscript on MacArthur that did not become publishable. An old publishing friend told me, with the elegance he always has shown in such matters, that the manuscript would have no interest for readers. I had been mistaken in thinking otherwise and not without hesitation took the advice. In this confusion the friends at the Foundation could not have been nicer.

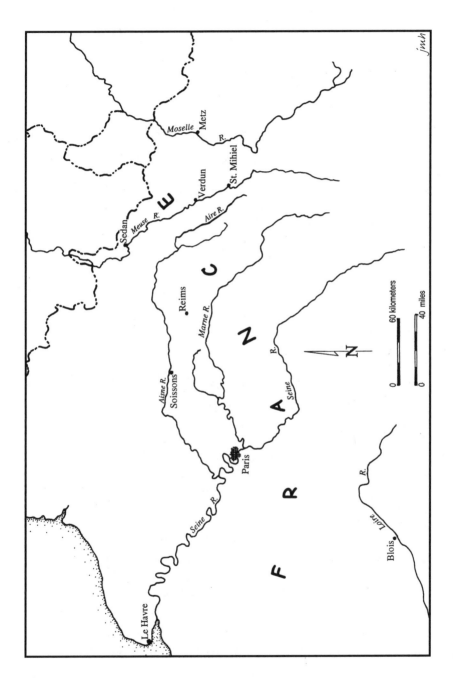

The Western Front

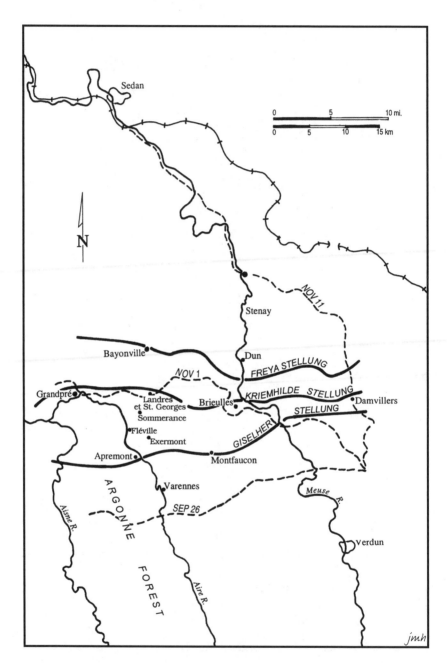

The Hindenburg Line

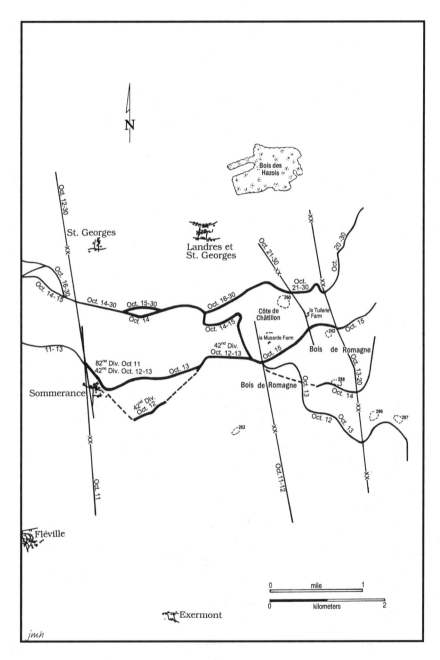

The Forty-second Division

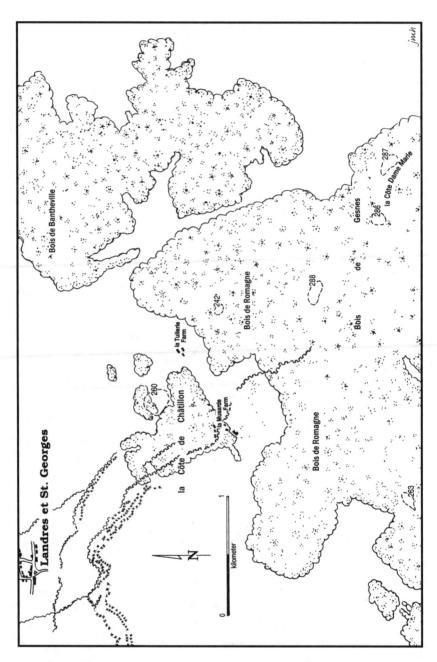

Côte de Châtillon

The Question of
MacArthur's Reputation

★

One

★ ★

PREPARATION

General Douglas MacArthur made his reputation from an action toward the end of the World War, on October 14–16, 1918: the taking of the Côte de Châtillon, which broke the German main battle line on the Western Front. Few Americans at the time, and even fewer as the years passed and Douglas MacArthur's name became known everywhere in the country, could have related what happened in the taking of this hill in northern France. Almost no one could have told what MacArthur did at this crucial time. He was hailed as a hero, yet many others who fought during those three days could with more justification have been hailed as such. How did MacArthur end up with a reputation as a leader of men in battle, without actually leading his men in battle?

The purpose of what follows is to set it all out. The sending of the American Expeditionary Forces (AEF) to France is a story in itself, a massive achievement of the AEF's commander in chief, General John J. Pershing, together with the army's chief of staff in Washington, General Peyton C. March, the latter officer often left out of the organizational equation. The AEF entered the Western Front gradually in the spring and summer of 1918, then massively in an action of little moment at St. Mihiel where the German

Army was about to leave a salient southeast of Verdun. Two weeks later, on September 26, the army took the field in full force, in the great battle of the Meuse-Argonne. Here was the largest battle in American history, in which 1.3 million men took part. It was the most costly battle as well—twenty-six thousand men died and tens of thousands were wounded. The next most costly battle in the nation's history was Okinawa in 1945, with fourteen thousand dead, five thousand of them aboard U.S. Navy ships struck by Japanese kamikaze planes. In the Meuse-Argonne the U.S. Army made a series of attacks. The first was the battle's opening; the second began on October 4. Both were failures. The third opened on October 14, and it was in this attack that Châtillon played a major part. The action at the Côte de Châtillon thus represented a poised moment, with the huge battle seeming to hinge on its success. The troops of General MacArthur attacked at a time when an ambitious commander, if successful, could make a reputation.

1

The cause of America's entrance into the World War was the act of the Imperial German Government in instituting unrestricted ("sink on sight") submarine warfare in the sea approaches to the British Isles. The administration of President Woodrow Wilson broke formal diplomatic relations and waited to see if the Germans were serious. They were, and Wilson declared war, after a congressional vote in favor, on April 6, 1917.[1] Immediately thereafter came one of the important preliminaries of the battle of the Meuse-Argonne: a dual failure by the administration in, first, providing transportation and weapons for the AEF and, second, organizing the decrepit War Department in Washington for war.

The failure to mobilize American industry was serious, for the greatest industrial nation in the world, which America had become in the 1880s, produced neither ships to take the AEF to France nor weapons with which the troops might fight. Ship production in 1917–1918 was a complete failure. The United States had once been one of the Western world's greatest sea powers, due to the easy availability of timber. But when iron and steel ships replaced the wooden ships of time immemorial, markedly after the American Civil War, the European nations took the lead in shipbuilding because of their easy access to iron ore and much cheaper labor. As a result, the Americans had the same tonnage of oceangoing ships in 1917—that is, one million tons—as they had had just before the War of 1812. In remedying this situation, the Wilson administration, despite its national program in 1916 known as "preparedness," which was an election program for the Democratic president that year, had done virtually nothing. The administration's efforts over the next months in 1917 were of no avail. The U.S. shipbuilding program did not get into high gear until the summer of 1918, when the first ship of a projected two hundred was launched at a huge new shipyard in what had been a muddy flat near Philadelphia. The ship and its successors did not get fitted out until after the war was over. Meanwhile, German submarines were sinking vast numbers of Allied ships until the British government instituted convoys, and the latter diminished the availability of ships because all had to sail together, which required ships to sit idle waiting for convoys at designated ports.

The ship story was a tragedy for the organization of the American Army in northern France because it meant that when the AEF was transported to France beginning in February and March 1918, there was no room either for trucks or for the more conventional, for that time, means of transportation, horses and mules. Thus, the AEF had to make do with what meager supplies of animal transport were available in western Europe, leaving the AEF short of transportation in the Meuse-Argonne. Often quarter-horsepower prime movers, which were soldiers, handled transportation. There were stories of divisions, and it apparently happened with at least one, that dragged their own artillery pieces along the inadequate French roads, getting them to the front. Too, if American trucks, easily available from the factories in Detroit, could have been substituted for animal transport, the tens of thousands of soldiers necessary to care for the animals could have turned their attention to more military tasks.

Just as the Wilson administration in Washington botched the ship program, so it failed in the production of weapons. Even though none of the weapons needed by the troops in France were available in quantity in April 1917, they might have been produced, quickly, in time for troop use. The list began with airplanes, at the time of value for reconnaissance and artillery spotting; the administration's plane program, much bragged about, completely failed, with nothing being available before the war's end. More important was the failure of the most important weapon for war in 1917–1918, which was artillery. The army sought, foolishly, to reproduce French artillery, heavy and light, the latter including the vaunted French 75s. The 75s were fine guns, equal to those of the British and German armies, but they had been made by artisans, and the effort to turn them out in American factories required the most difficult of measurements, involving conversions from the metric system to feet and yards and pounds. This effort failed to make American reproductions of either heavy artillery pieces, 155s, or the light pieces available before the armistice in 1918, which of course was too late for the troops. All the while the U.S. Army had available a quite acceptable light artillery piece, dating from 1902, which it could have mass-produced. As for production of heavy artillery—the 155 mm pieces used for long-range firing—rifles, and howitzers (the latter have a lower muzzle velocity and deliver curved fire), it ran into different troubles, and similarly failed. Tank production was an abject failure. No more ammunition—shells and powder and cartridges—came from American factories in 1917–1918 than had in 1914–1917. Springfield rifles, splendid weapons, could be produced only in army arsenals and were unavailable in sufficient quantities, forcing the army to adapt an inferior British rifle for Springfield ammunition. Only with machine guns did the army gain production of fine guns, those both heavy and light of the inventor Browning. But they were not available until the last weeks of the war, leaving the AEF with the unsatisfactory Chauchat for a light gun, arguably the worst machine gun on the Western Front, and the French heavy Hotchkiss, which was better.

For the most part, French equipment substituted for the lacking American equipment, which spoke a great deal for the ability of the tightly controlled French economy to produce war materials. The AEF was grateful for the planes, artillery, tanks, and even the Chauchat submachine gun, which was better than nothing, but not much, for it periodically jammed. The procurement officers at Pershing's headquarters would have done better to take, if they could get them, British Lewis guns, equal to the German Maxims. But the awkwardness of being an orphan army asking for what equipment it could obtain was that in several categories it did not get the kind it wanted. In others, such as planes and artillery, it did not get enough. The AEF needed more planes. In artillery it could have used twice as many pieces as the French gave the divisions, although it is likely that if the guns had been available they would have received indifferent use in many of the American artillery brigades (each division had an artillery brigade of three twelve-hundred-man regiments, one with heavy guns, the other two with light).

These failures in the production of ships and weapons must, unfortunately, be laid at the door of the administration of President Wilson. The sad truth is that the wartime president, who cut a most attractive figure as he stood before the House and Senate, who was capable of the most inspiring of speeches, was a poor organizer of the war effort in terms of what the AEF needed for its most pressing test on the battlefield, the difficult contest with the German Army in the Meuse-Argonne.

The other large failure of the Wilson administration, until the appearance of General March in Washington early in 1918, in what few months remained for his leadership, was in the necessary reorganization of the War Department.[2] Beginning in 1916, the department was under the direction of Secretary of War Newton D. Baker, a former student of President Wilson when the president was Professor Wilson and taught a course in public administration at Johns Hopkins University, near his regular teaching institution at Princeton. The secretary's qualification for his department was the mayoralty of Cleveland, which was no qualification at all. Arriving in Washington, he had the quaint notion that he should not interfere in military matters, as they were the business of the military; for this total lack of understanding of his duties he explained himself with references to the Civil War and the tendency, which Baker discerned as wrong, of President Jefferson Davis of the Confederate States of America to interfere in the command problems of General Robert E. Lee. The result of this understanding of a war in 1861–1865 that was almost completely unlike that of 1917–1918 was that Baker tolerated three incompetent chiefs of staff (one of whom was an acting chief) before, in perhaps the single inspired action of his secretaryship, he chose Peyton March early in 1918. The War Department did not get off dead center until then, did not manage much more than the introduction, through the president and Congress, of a draft, the construction of vast cantonments, and the bringing of the National Guard and tens of thousands of civilians into the camps in the autumn and winter of 1917–1918. There the members of the Guard and the levies of new men barely organized themselves into divisions before it became necessary to send them to France.

General March saw the need for troops abroad. When his AEF counterpart, the commander in France, Pershing, saw the opportunity and took it of using British and some French ships to help bring over the AEF in the early spring and summer of 1918, March moved with the extraordinary resolution of which he was capable. He sent the divisions in their tens of thousands of troops, eventually hundreds of thousands. By the time of the armistice Pershing had more than two million men, with 1.3 million in the Meuse-Argonne, a major achievement of those two able generals.[3]

Where the work of March in assisting Pershing could not succeed, for time did not allow it, was in training the troops he sent over. Many of the new divisions of National Army troops—that is, draft men, as opposed to National Guard troops or Regular divisions (consisting of a core of Regular officers, and sometimes little more than that)—were not trained in much more than close-order drill, together with the elementary construction of trenches, as if that prepared a soldier for anything. They were trained in bayonet practice, which looked efficient because it appeared ferocious. General Robert L. Bullard in 1917 filled his notes with commentaries of how use of the bayonet taught a soldier to be ferocious. In reality the bayonet was completely outmoded once the German Army opened its great spring and summer offensive in 1918 and turned trench warfare into open warfare. U.S. Army officers often spoke of training men to be soldiers, by which they also meant saluting, a nineteenth-century exercise of no importance for the divisions en route to France. But such was as far as many of the divisions had gotten. When the Meuse-Argonne opened, the troops on the line were largely untrained. They learned to fight with what one might describe as German efficiency—for the German Army was the most efficient in Europe—only over the next weeks. This learning was costly in casualties, for the Meuse-Argonne cost the lives of twenty-six thousand men and tens of thousands of wounded.[4]

General Pershing often complained about the work of his counterpart in the United States, General March, and complained about training, undertaking an entirely new training program for the four divisions he possessed over the winter of 1917–1918, the First, Second, Twenty-sixth, and Forty-second. As the new divisions came over he sought to retrain them, carefully counting—his assistants of course did the counting—the numbers of days they spent in this or that series of exercises, comparing them to his four winter divisions. He established a series of schools and sought attendance by officers and men, in more than a few cases so disrupting the training of those who were not called to the schools that not much was accomplished.

Of the problems suffered by the AEF, training was assuredly at the front of the list, but there was also the problem of replacements. While the divisions were preparing to go overseas, they suffered massive influxes of replacements, disorganizing what little training the men had received. Once in France, they obtained more replacements because of losses in battle or due to illness. The new men often had no training, and many had just entered the army, some with two or three weeks of service before finding themselves overseas. The Forty-second Division, one of the four that Pershing had over the winter of 1917–1918, received altogether, at home and abroad, twenty thousand replacements. Its authorized strength was twenty-eight thousand. Lieutenant Colonel William J. Donovan of the 165th New York Regiment estimated that his regiment, which he took against the German line on October 14–15, 1918, was 50 percent recruits from a few weeks before. In daylight the recruits through lack of training were likely to bunch, to group together, sensing that to be close to other men meant better protection—when instead it only provided better targets for German machine gunners and artillery batteries. There was consideration of night attacks by some regiments, and reconsideration because such attacks could not hold together if the troops had newly joined their regiments. Quite beyond the high casualties among recruits thrown into serious fighting, there was a marked loss of noncommissioned officers, the sergeants and corporals, killed or wounded in their efforts to keep recruits from bunching.

In organizing the AEF a special problem was the size of the units, which General Pershing resolved in his own way. Unfortunately, his resolution did not turn out very well. For division size he opted for units of twice and more the size of the Allied and German divisions. As mentioned, the size of each division was twenty-eight thousand men, with two infantry brigades of eight thousand each, each brigade containing two infantry regiments of four thousand. The regiments contained three battalions, of one thousand men each, and each battalion four companies of two hundred fifty men each. Each company had four platoons of sixty, and each platoon four squads of fifteen. It was symmetrical enough, but the size of the units was large, probably too large, for it led to unwieldiness, with many commanders having more men than they could handle. German commanders thought the Americans inclined to mass tactics, true enough of the recruits, and further true in terms of unit size. The presumption of observers was that the AEF opted for huge units because the Regular Army possessed only six thousand officers at the time of the declaration of war, so that the scarcity of officers was a large problem. Another theory, often heard, was that the large unit size allowed for replacements, with each division and its subunits able to handle losses. This theory was less believable than the preceding one, for it soon was necessary to cannibalize some of the divisions that came over. The AEF's replacements were so many, and the need for replacements was so large, that the army was still only beginning to get itself organized when the war came to an end.

At the outset of the battle of the Meuse-Argonne there were so many problems in the AEF that Pershing, riding in his staff car, unconsciously spoke one day to himself, overheard by an assistant, relating that he did not know how he could go on. For the most part, and this utterance was almost the only sign of irresolution that escaped him, he and his assistants carried on.

Also relevant are the AEF's strategy and tactics as they developed in the summer and autumn of 1918 when the Americans went into action. Pershing and a small group of officers came over to France in May 1917, followed by the First Division, a select organization of officers and men from the small groupings that constituted the Regular Army. Having arrived, and after a headquarters colonel in a piece of oratory told a group of Parisians at Lafayette's tomb on July 4, 1917, "Lafayette, we are here," the AEF's commander in chief established himself at a French barracks town, Chaumont. His staff officers quickly made a decision to concentrate the divisions, when they arrived, at the far right of the Allied line, with the British taking the part of the line closest to the Channel, the French the middle (the approaches to Paris), and the AEF the area east of the Meuse and Verdun, principally Lorraine but also Alsace, including the mountains down to Switzerland. The far right of the line held an advantage for supply, as it did not interfere with supply of the British Army nor of the French in the middle. It allowed the Americans use of the underemployed southern ports, where they could establish their own supply organizations, which gradually amounted to a vast profusion of warehouses, and reinforce with gigantic cranes the antediluvian loading facilities of those ports. They could also reorganize the French railroads with their small freight cars and "40 and 8s," so-called because they could carry forty men or eight horses.

There was a second advantage in taking the right-hand portion of the line from the Channel to Switzerland. It put the Americans close to the German fortress of Metz, a crucial place in the German line. If the line could be turned, as the Americans fondly wished to do (this hope was known as "the Metz strategy"), it might allow them to enter more quickly into Germany and disrupt, indeed break, the German supply system. That system ran by rail northwestward through Sedan and Mézières into what had been in 1914–1917 the much more active portion of the Western Front (the American sector as chosen by the AEF had been a rest area).[5]

The Metz strategy dominated American military thinking until the new Allied commander in chief, Marshal Ferdinand Foch, almost suddenly, early in September 1918, persuaded Pershing to accept a new place for battle, what became the Meuse-Argonne. By that time Pershing's troops were already gathered before the German salient at St. Mihiel and prepared to strike on September 12. Many of them had planned on what their commander looked forward to, a continuation of the attack in the direction of Metz. With acceptance of the Meuse-Argonne, which evidently pleased Foch because it brought AEF troops closer to the sectors of the French and British in what the ebullient marshal described as "all the world to the battle," it was necessary to break off the attack after pushing in the St. Mihiel salient, which the AEF did with overwhelming force, two hundred twenty-five thousand troops against twenty-five thousand German defenders (who were actually moving back of their own volition when the Americans attacked). To the disappointment of the army, the commander in chief directed a breaking off and moved the troops forty or fifty miles to the west to the new place of attack.

It is an open question as to whether St. Mihiel should have been undertaken when the Meuse-Argonne loomed, just two weeks after the St. Mihiel attack. Whatever we think in retrospect, it was undertaken, with the result that many of the troops who participated in the Meuse-Argonne's first attack came into the sector after walking the distance, or being gathered up in primitive French trucks, known as *camions,* and riding the distance on the floorboards, without springs, which was almost as bad as walking. The artillery and trains—supply, ammunition, sanitary (medical)—had to go the distance on meandering roads. Animals made the distance under intense difficulty, often without oats and hay, and thousands starved. The new offensive opened on time, but the troops were tired from the journey and in poor physical condition from waiting in wet forests and often, in addition, enduring shell fire during the wait.

As for the AEF's tactics, the less said about them the better, for they revealed, especially among the higher officers, little knowledge of European tactical solutions.[6] What happened with the officers of the Regular Army—and all of the divisional commanders save one, the National Guard major general of the Twenty-seventh Division, were Regular Army men—was that this select group of higher officers took their tactics from their own experience. Merely to recite the places where they had fought shows how out of date and irrelevant those tactics were. The primary experience was in the Philippines, where the warfare of the Insurrection and of the Moro campaigns of subsequent years was so unlike the warfare of the Western Front as to be ludicrous. Nonetheless, time after time, the ranking officers of the AEF referred their auditors or observers to what they had learned in the islands. General MacArthur served three times in the Philippines. Renowned even in 1918 for his soliloquies on tactics, also strategy, he could only have learned these ways of war from the Philippine tours. If there were other reference points for AEF officers of the Regular Army, they were the smaller forays in Central America and the Caribbean or, for those individuals closer to Pershing, the experience in the Mexican Punitive Expedition in 1916–1917, of no more relevance than the Philippines.

Given this lack of European experience, there might have been intense study of what happened in Europe in 1914–1917 (or for that matter what happened in the Russo-Japanese War of 1904–1905 and the Balkan wars just before the World War). But the army was not a place for theoretical study, and when the Leavenworth Schools were established by the lawyer Elihu Root, secretary of war after the administrative failures of the Spanish-American War, their field of study was the Franco-Prussian War—which presented some advantage in terms of geography but almost none in regard to tactics. The graduates of Leavenworth learned how to write orders and simulate command of large units, but there was an unreal aspect to these studies that never escaped them, making a later student of what happened at Leavenworth wonder if the training there amounted to much.[7] The War College established in Washington by Secretary Root was so small an organization that it had little effect upon the army, one way or another. The residential buildings for generals and colonels possessed fine Grecian columns, and the houses were probably fun to live in, but the college was not a college in any other respect, only a group of officers gathered in Washington, most of whom were delegated to various parts of the War Department, where they performed whatever tasks came their way.

Another course the army might have taken was not merely to send attachés to the several war ministries of the European powers, so that they might follow the procedures of the national armies, but to take to heart the tactical lessons those national posts offered. The army sent the attachés, but when the latter sent back reports, in whatever detail, the officials at the War College did not read them. They arranged them in piles, and nothing more happened. When a junior officer, a member of the general staff (although that meant little or nothing), sought to arrange dissemination of the reports, there was an accidental disclosure of a minor item that a British officer believed to represent a failure by the Americans to respect British secrets, and there was no more dissemination of attachés' reports.[8]

All this meant that in many of the actions that were part of the first three U.S. Army attacks in the Meuse-Argonne prior to the immensely successful attack of November 1, the AEF blundered and barely moved forward to the second line of German defense, the Kriemhilde Stellung. The latter was a cunning combination of barbed wire, machine guns in trenches or cement pillboxes, and exceedingly well placed artillery, a combination never seen in the Philippines. These defenses were virtually impregnable, unless fortune or a wise infantry commander arranged tactics to allow an AEF success, which is what happened in the taking of the Côte de Châtillon.

In the first AEF attack in the Meuse-Argonne a huge artillery bombardment lasting three hours surprised the German defenders and presaged an infantry attack. At 5:30 a.m. the bombardment turned into a rolling barrage, and the divisions went forward. At first it was easy going, with advances of three to five miles to the north, into German-held territory. But by the end of the second day, September 27, the defenders had brought in more troops and begun putting their artillery in play. The German artillery was successful in part because the troops that had occupied this area for four years, since 1914, knew the locations of all the villages and crossroads, and in part because the German air force, skilled in working with infantry, hovered over American lines and radioed the locations of all attractive targets. German pilots came out of clouds and pounced on American observation balloons, sending them down in flames, the observers in parachutes if they were fortunate enough to escape the flaming mass of balloon debris descending above them. The wise inspector of the three left-hand divisions on the American line, Colonel Lesley J. McNair, wrote that the American artillery was poorly directed, much of its fire on so-called targets of opportunity, which meant firing blindly, hoping to score worthwhile hits. Infantry, the colonel thought, was poorly handled, without any sense of the need to hurry before the enemy brought up reinforcements; the infantry of the Seventy-seventh Division, whose task was to clear out the upper half of the Argonne Forest, "sauntered" into the forest. The result was that the fighting arm of Pershing's Chaumont headquarters, First Army as the general denominated it, was stopped everywhere by September 28 or 29. In one instance, the Thirty-fifth Division, third from the left of the line, was turned back by the Germans, who retook territory the German Army had lost and nearly forced the division down to where it had started on "D" Day and "H" Hour.[9] Two or three other divisions in line did nearly as badly, causing Pershing to bring them out for the second AEF attack, replacing them with what he hoped were better commanded units.

After a bare few days of rest, insufficient to do much more than move out the failing divisions, the next attack, October 4, started again with artillery fire. In contrast to the initial attack, the infantry did not get more than a few hundred yards ahead of the line of September 28–29. The troops were tired. Some of their commanders proved no better than those of divisions that had done poorly before. In the second attack the only tactic of distinction came when the commander of I Corps, General Liggett (Seventy-seventh, Twenty-eighth, and First divisions), sent a brigade of his reserve division, the Eighty-second, up the corps's single highway of importance, the French Route Nationale 46, which passed north alongside the Aire River until that river met the small town of Fléville near the top of the Argonne (whereupon the Aire turned northwest until it reached Grandpré). Using a ford in the Aire, the Eighty-second's regiments turned left into the Argonne, threatened German forces to the south and west, some of which had cut off a battalion of the Seventy-seventh Division, the "Lost Battalion," freed the battalion's dwindling force, and together with the First Division that replaced the Thirty-fifth drove German units north to their main line of defense, the Kriemhilde Stellung.

General Pershing made himself an army group commander on October 12 by appointing the commander of I Corps, Liggett, in his place at First Army and creating Second Army, at the outset a skeleton organization under General Bullard. Liggett did not take up his new command until the conclusion of Pershing's third attack in the Meuse-Argonne, that of October 14, in which the brigade of General MacArthur distinguished itself.

2

It was on the night of October 11–12 that the Forty-second Division entered the line in the Meuse-Argonne, replacing the First Division, which in turn had replaced the failed Thirty-fifth. The Forty-second was a National Guard division composed of units from twenty-six states and the District of Columbia. Present in the War Department when the division was organized, the then Major MacArthur said to Secretary Baker, quite appropriately, "It will stretch across the country like a rainbow," and thereby gave the Forty-second its name of Rainbow Division.[10]

To follow the First Division was an honor, for the First had the reputation of being the best division in the AEF. It had been the initial division to be organized and had the choice of officers in the Regular Army, and its non-commissioned officers had enjoyed whatever experiences Regulars could take from their Philippine, Caribbean, and Mexican assignments. In the Meuse-Argonne the First had done a magnificent piece of work by pushing the boundaries of First Army north, taking Fléville on the initial day of action, sending its regiments east as far as they could go to hold a line even with Fléville at the west of its sector.

It was a place of honor to follow the First Division, but two fateful accompaniments made this assignment of questionable value. One was the Forty-second's new corps commander, Major General Charles P. Summerall, whom General Pershing elevated from command of the First Division. He possessed judgment as an artillery officer. Artillery was his specialty, but his ability as an infantry commander was doubtful. After an awkward start with the First Division in July, he took firm control of the division and could push it in almost any direction he wished. But he did not care if the pushing was at a high cost in casualties. In the days from October 4 until his division's relief by the Forty-second, he nearly broke the First, by some counts losing eleven thousand men, by others between seven and eight thousand, the highest division loss in the Meuse-Argonne. It presaged what he might ask of the Forty-second when he was elevated to command of V Corps on October 12.

Another omen for the Forty-second's officers and men was Pershing's decision to make V Corps's left-hand division, the Forty-second, a part of his main attack on October 14, together with the Fifth Division, the left-hand division of III Corps to the right of V Corps. This was a large assignment. The other division of V Corps, the Thirty-second, the National Guard division of Michigan and Wisconsin, was to conduct a holding action while the Forty-second and Fifth thrust ahead in a gigantic pincers that would come together above the Thirty-second, above the place that had stalled the Wolverines, as the Thirty-second's men called themselves. This was the Côte Dame Marie, a crescent-shaped height in their territory that had defied capture, facing a plain with little place to protect attacking infantry. The crescent had virtual clifflike walls and hills at each tip and faced to the south, commanding all the plain within sight. Presumably the Forty-second's and Fifth's regiments, encircling it to the north, could take it at leisure from the rear.[11]

The Forty-second, coming into the Meuse-Argonne under a new and untried corps commander, found itself in a tactical complexity that was a good deal larger than its officers and men understood. The proposed pincers relied on cooperation with the Fifth Division, a unit that the Forty-second knew little about. Its own staff officers in division headquarters then elaborated a plan of attack, Field Order 36, that similarly relied on teamwork, this time not between divisions but between the Forty-second's two infantry brigades, the Eighty-third under Brigadier General Michael J. Lenihan and the Eighty-fourth to its right under General MacArthur. The plan was for all four infantry regiments of the division to attack abreast, with Lenihan's 166th Ohio on the left and his 165th New York to its right. Next was MacArthur's 167th Alabama Regiment, and to the far right was his 168th Iowa. The Kriemhilde Stellung, however, was not a straight line. At first it went along to the east at the top of the division's sector, just below villages by the names of St. Georges and Landres et St. Georges. The Eighty-third Brigade would move directly north against the line. In the sector of the Eighty-fourth Brigade lay the Côte de Châtillon, a hill in the shape of a triangle resting on one tip, and the line followed the hill down to the tip, ascending on the northeast side, forcing MacArthur's brigade to attack Châtillon from its northwest and northeast faces. In the attack of the Forty-second's four infantry regiments, it was necessary for those of MacArthur's Eighty-fourth to attack first, so as to prevent German machine guns and artillery on Châtillon from enfilading, firing from the right, on Lenihan's two regiments of the Eighty-third.

The Forty-second's attack plan allowed for MacArthur's brigade to take Châtillon before Lenihan's Eighty-third Brigade moved out. It gave the Eighty-fourth an entirely insufficient time to complete that task, however: three hours, between 5:30 and 8:30 a.m. on October 14. The time was insufficient because Châtillon contained deep wire on its northwest face, two widths of twenty or more feet each, behind which was a tank trap, with machine guns on an elevated step. On the hill, with excellent observation of where the Eighty-third Brigade would move forward, were carefully sited artillery pieces. Below Châtillon were its outer defenses, two fortified groups of farm buildings, Musarde and Tuilerie, and below them two hills protected by machine guns, a hill numbered 288, heavily protected, and above it a lesser hill, 242.

The Forty-second Division had two days, Saturday, October 12, and Sunday, October 13, to prepare itself for a plan that was too complicated, and in its complexity included an impossibly short length of time for its right-hand infantry brigade, MacArthur's Eighty-fourth, to take a most carefully defended position. Yet taking that position was necessary to protect the Eighty-fourth's fellow brigade, the Eighty-third, as it moved north, three hours later, to take the German line below the two villages.

The complexity of the Forty-second's attack plan, and within it the inadequacies, raises a question about the division's leading officers, notably the commander, Major General Frank T. Menoher. General Menoher looked more like a general than did most of the AEF's commanders, for he was thin and athletic, as opposed to the usual avoirdupois of major generals. Like several of Pershing's leading commanders, he was one of his classmates from the West Point class of 1886. His career had not been exceptional, and he had moved upward in rank at the usual slow Regular speed, neither rapidly nor remarkably. He was in Cuba during the war with Spain and had three tours in the Philippines. Promoted to colonel in 1916, he was elevated in August 1917, like most Regular colonels, to brigadier general, and a few months later to major general and command of the Forty-second. He seemed well liked, but it was difficult to know what his officers and men admired. He was perhaps, if one may use the word, inoffensive. Some years later Pershing, evaluating the army's generals at that time, found him easygoing and without initiative.[12] Having known him at West Point, the commander in chief might have anticipated that quality and headed him off to a supply depot or a safe headquarters slot in Great Britain, rather than keeping him in France, where he was unsafe in command. There was an indefinable something about Menoher that was unremarkable.

The trouble with the Forty-second Division's command structure was more the inability of the general in charge of the Eighty-third Brigade, Lenihan. Commanding a brigade in which one of its regiments, the 165th New York, was so strongly Irish and Catholic, especially its Third Battalion, the Shamrock Battalion, known for its origin in New York's famed Fighting Sixty-ninth Regiment that traced back to the Civil War, he might have seemed the right man in the right place. He often helped the regiment's chaplain, Francis P. Duffy, serve Mass. He had been with the brigade since its organization and had a long and honorable background as a Regular since graduation from West Point in 1887. The trouble was that over the many years he had cultivated indecision as a way of surviving the small-unit (for Regular units in peacetime were all small) feuds, and the higher he rose the less he decided.

Lenihan was taciturn to a fault. Colonel Henry J. Reilly took his place when the corps commander, Summerall, relieved Lenihan on the second night after the attack, after the Eighty-third had failed against its objective. Reilly remembered a meeting on the evening of Sunday, October 13, the night before the attack, that was also attended by the colonel of the 165th New York, Harry D. Mitchell, and the colonel of Lenihan's other infantry regiment, the 166th Ohio, a thoughtful and quick-witted Columbus lawyer, Benson W. Hough. The colonels went from their units to the general's command post in a shack near Exermont, through the increasing dusk, in the rain, encountering innumerable bodies of Thirty-fifth and First Division men who had fallen in past days and lay in the mud unburied. It was all they could do to avoid stepping on the pitiful and putrefying remains. Arriving at the brigade command post they looked over the attack plan for the brigade for the next morning, October 14. The task ahead of them was a major one, with the troops needing to walk forward largely through open fields, toward the German main line ahead. Wire, machine guns, and sited artillery would stare the regiments virtually in the face, with the villages of St. Georges and Landres et St. Georges on the far side, the goal being to take the line and advance not merely to the villages but beyond a mile or so, all during that morning. In conference one of General Lenihan's colonels asked what would happen if the Eighty-fourth Brigade did not take Châtillon by 8:30, H Hour for the Eighty-third's regiments. To this prescient query the brigadier of the Eighty-third made no reply. The colonels left the shack on the hillside near Exermont and found dusk turning into near dark, the task of avoiding unburied bodies more awkward. Reilly thought it all resembled one of the British painter William Orpen's shadowy landscapes, perhaps a painting of a frigate or a ship-of-the-line lying in still waters, sails furled, guns rolled back.[13]

The Forty-second's other infantry brigade commander, MacArthur, was a marked contrast to Lenihan. From birth he seemed fated to be a general; his father had been a general. Much younger than Lenihan, he had graduated from West Point in 1903 as first captain, head of that year's corps of cadets. He spent time in the Philippines as a junior engineer officer. In 1913 he was assigned to the War Department, where, like other members of the general staff, he engaged in a variety of tasks. For a few weeks during the occupation of Veracruz in 1914 he undertook a special mission, for which he was recommended for the Congressional Medal of Honor (he did not obtain it). One of his tasks was acting as the War Department press officer. In 1917, during a organization of the Forty-second Division under command of the department's general in charge of National Guard activities, he joined the division as its chief of staff with the rank of colonel. In the summer of 1918, when command of the Eighty-fourth Brigade became available, he became its brigadier general.

The work of getting the four regiments of the two brigades in place had, for the most part, not proved difficult, save in the instance of the 168th Iowa Regiment. The Eighty-third Brigade line, inherited from the regiments of the First Division, had been clearly defined, and Lenihan's men simply had moved up. On MacArthur's side the Alabama troops had little trouble, shielded by the Bois de Romagne and the tendency of the German defenders above to stay there, to the north of the woods. But the Iowa regiment was the division's far right unit and had to adjust its sector to that of the V Corps's other division, the Thirty-second. An order came through on the morning of October 13 for the 168th to move its line nearly a kilometer, three-fifths of a mile, to the east, and the battalions moved without telling their companion regiment, the 167th; the 167th had to feel for its new line and found that, in the meantime, barely a few hours, German patrols were feeling down into the area. The 168th's move—it was a tangled situation—was caused by the Thirty-second Division's need to take the Côte Dame Marie; it was so engrossed by the task that its far left regiment, the 127th, could not manage the posting, either with patrols or companies, of its area toward the 168th.

Word for the 168th to move came in, and the commander who had to do it was the major of the First Battalion, which had already been designated the attack battalion for the next day. Fortunately Major Lloyd D. Ross, who came from the town of Red Oak, Iowa, and was to star in the subsequent movements of the 168th until the taking of Châtillon on October 16, was equal to the work at hand. Ross had joined the Iowa militia in 1893. When Company M, his National Guard company, was brought into national service in 1898 and sent to the Philippines, he was caught up in the tedium of parts of that operation, which involved pacification of the insurrection. First, he and the company suffered the long voyage out. Then they were sent to rescue a Spanish garrison on Panay surrounded by *insurrectos*. All the while he remained aboard ship, perhaps the longest ordeal aboard a transport at that time. He took part in the later actions against the insurrection, returning home to Iowa via Japan late in 1899. He thereafter continued what became forty-seven years in the federal service with the militia or Guard, from which he retired in 1940.[14]

Major Ross, as he became in September 1918, was a natural soldier, a man of great judgment who could control sizable bodies of troops. Despite the

fact that he nominally commanded only the First Battalion, he was denominated commander of the 168th's front line by the commander of the 168th,
Lieutenant Colonel Matthew B. Tinley. That gave Ross control over the regiment's other two battalions, on which he could call for reinforcements, taking say, all four companies of the Second Battalion, merely informing
Captain Glenn C. Haynes without going through regimental headquarters
and Lieutenant Colonel Tinley.

When Ross found out about moving to the right he sensed that, despite
his somewhat casual instruction from division to reconnoiter the area, division might not know much of anything about what was there. He sent a sizable group of scouts under his battalion intelligence officer, Captain
Raymond Turner. Turner took Sergeant John Fleming and seventeen other
men together with Lieutenant Spalding and several noncommissioned officers from Companies C and D, which were to occupy this area.[15] Going into
the Bois de Gesnes, southeast of the Bois de Romagne, they went north up to
the base of Hill 288, to see if the Germans were there. Division intelligence
said they were not, that the hill was occupied by the 127th Regiment of the
Thirty-second Division. Turner and his men worked their way west until
they came to the road that ran above 288.

At this juncture matters became interesting. Fleming and five scouts went
forward, cautiously, with the others back fifty yards so as not to make the
force seem overwhelming in the event a few Germans came up. The force had
not gone more than a hundred yards before a machine gun opened fire. The
first burst killed two men. The others scattered. A party of perhaps twenty-
five Germans, lying in ambush beside the road, fired on Fleming and one of
the advance scouts, mortally wounding the latter. Fleming dragged the scout
into a small hole, but several Germans pounced on him and knocked him
unconscious with a rifle butt, taking both of the Americans prisoner. The
scout died a few days later. Fleming came back to the Forty-second after the
war, and Captain Turner talked with him. He said he had been closely questioned for several days by German intelligence officers, then threatened, the
proceedings brought to an end by an officer who gripped him on the back
and said, "You're a damned good soldier."

What the reconnaissance showed was that division did not know the
lines. This meant two things. For one, if Ross had sent a scout or two into
the area he might have received them back with word, totally untrue, that
the area was unoccupied, and the entire First Battalion would have been

trapped. The G-2 of the division, Lieutenant Colonel Noble B. Judah, was incompetent, and of course overranked, as were all the division officers numbered in accord with General Pershing's G system installed in the sections at headquarters in Chaumont and in those of First Army (G-1 personnel, G-2 intelligence, G-3 operations, G-4 supply, G-5 training). There is no evidence that Judah went up to the line to see what was there. In the course of the operation to capture Châtillon he announced in his intelligence analysis that the Forty-second Division faced twenty-three German divisions and nineteen independent units, when in fact it faced the German Forty-first Division, under full strength with a reported twenty-five men to each infantry company, but protected by its position behind the Kriemhilde Stellung, by its wire and machine guns, and by its artillery in Châtillon and in the Bois des Hazois above Landres et St. Georges. Part of another division, and Judah did not know this, came into the Forty-second's sector early on the morning of October 14. That was all, Judah to the contrary. The lack of intelligence at division headquarters was never the subject of investigation.

It is entirely possible that division was acting on Colonel Judah's intelligence that Hill 288 was in friendly hands when it assigned the Eighty-fourth Brigade the impossible task of taking Hill 288 as well as the smaller hill directly above it numbered 242 and the two fortified groups of farm buildings next to the Côte de Châtillon, Musarde and Tuilerie, and Châtillon itself—all to be accomplished between the hours of 5:30 and 8:30 A.M. But then the expectation of taking so much territory in three hours was so preposterous that control of 288 would have made no difference.[16]

Two

★ ★

OCTOBER 14

An almost open difference in the command calculations between generals on the one side and colonels or lesser regimental commanders on the other appeared at the outset of the action of the Forty-second Division on October 14. This difference became ever more evident as the action continued until its triumphant close, the taking of the Côte de Châtillon two days later, on October 16. It was a curious pattern, worthy not merely of mention but of analysis. This was the tendency of the generals to make tactical decisions and give tactical advice without thinking it through—offering it, to use the commonplace explanation, off the tops of their heads. On the part of regimental officers, the tactical decisions necessarily—so they believed—partook of front-line experience. No colonel or lieutenant colonel commanding a regiment or no major commanding a battalion would likely base his decisions on anything other than the exigencies of the moment. The behavior of the four regiments of the Forty-second Division, of their commanding officers as seen in the tactics of the battalions, could not afford to be careless, or to use another word common to eighteenth-century battlefields, gallant. Some years ago the military writer Walter Millis described how in the Spanish-American War an officer and his men could charge up a hill, the officer on a horse, holding his sword high in the air, his hat on the tip, his men following, everyone moving up toward certain death, and then surviving. In World War I, if they charged up a hill toward certain death, they received it.

There was an exception to the commonsensical approach of regimental commanders during the action of October 14–16, and that was the 165th New York Regiment, which for reasons best known to itself refused to display prudence, choosing the way of gallantry before the bristling defenses of the Kriemhilde Stellung. Why this happened defies easy analysis. It may have been that in moving forward against the enemy the 165th happened to be first and therefore bore the brunt of making an example—although the 165th's egregious losses occurred at a time when, battlefield information being slow in passing from unit to unit, the other regiments probably could not have profited from it. A possible reason the 165th New York did not learn the wisdom of prudence until the second day of the action, October 15, might have been its New York Catholic, largely Irish, makeup, as evidenced by the initial attack unit, the Third Battalion, the Shamrock Battalion based on the old Fighting Sixty-ninth Guard Regiment of Manhattan, which was so full of Irish names as to make one believe it had been constituted in the mother country. Years ago the Civil War historian Grady McWhiney elaborated a theory about why the Confederacy nearly outfought the much more powerful, in industrial base and population, Union. The South possessed a base, he wrote, of Celtic immigrants and—McWhiney was a fanatic on this point—their fighting spirit was a part of their being.[1] This theory has never seemed believable. McWhiney also argued that the shift in weaponry in the 1850s from muskets to rifles accounted in fair part for the sanguinary nature of the Civil War; the generals of the Union had grown up in the musket age when no musket bearer could hit a target until his enemy was within three hundred feet, and this made them oblivious to the danger of rifles.

1

General Summerall, the V Corps commander, maintained that every line of defense had a weak place, and the only way to find it was to attack along the full length of the line. For this reason, he approved the tactics of the Forty-second Division before the Kriemhilde Stellung, which were to attack on October 14 with all four regiments abreast. Summerall had done just that ten days before, on October 4, when in the AEF's second attack in the Meuse-Argonne he shoved his division into the German line with all four regiments abreast, and was so successful that General Pershing gave him command of the corps.

For the 165th the terrain to the north, over which the troops had to go, was forbidding. They would pass up out of the Bois de Maldah and Bois de Romagne, which allowed protection as they gathered to attack. Thereafter the 165th New York's sector was nearly level, a welcome surprise to the regiment that had fought across undulating and hilly country longer than it wished to remember. The terrain was open, save for small woods. The presumption was that the men could get across the open places. The way forward moved up to a brook, where it was a bit swampy. The land then rose gradually to the wire. A good road went from Sommerance, in the sector of the 166th Ohio, diagonally northeast to Landres et St. Georges. Because the road was cut below ground level, it became known as the sunken road. The decision was quickly taken to move the troops from the south, the woods of Maldah and Romagne, to a sort of way station at the brook where clumps of trees afforded protection against rifle and artillery fire, and then send them up to the wire and beyond.

The weather on the morning of October 14 was not cooperative. It was autumn in northern France, which meant rain and cold. It had rained all night and bade fair to rain all day. The men of the Forty-second had summer underwear and khaki clothing and carried single blankets, having dropped off their packs. They had no overcoats. Their army raincoats, poorly made, absorbed moisture. During the night of October 13–14 the men had tried to sleep in the mud, for there was nothing else with which to make a bed.

A sign of what was in store for the men of the 165th New York was the presence of Chaplain Duffy as they moved up. He stood on a small bluff and silently gave his blessing as the troops marched past. He wrote afterward that he did not need to speak as all around were fallen comrades from the Thirty-fifth Division and the First. German dead were there, too, but there were many more American graves, marked by rude crosses with dog tags nailed to them or sometimes by upturned rifles, with their bayonets stuck into the ground.[2]

The tactical arrangement was for General MacArthur's Eighty-fourth Brigade to attack first, to eliminate enfilading fire. The men did not know that the night before one of the colonels in conference with General Lenihan had asked if three hours was enough to achieve the brigade's objective.

The redoubtable Lieutenant Colonel Donovan, in charge of the front-line troops of the 165th, made some efforts to prepare his men for their ordeal. He told battalion commanders to have the men pick up extra bandoleers of cartridges, including bandoleers from dead men. Similarly, he ordered them to carry extra canteens, although those issued turned out to be French without cloth covers, so that the metal shone in the sunlight and made those carrying them instant targets for sharpshooters. Donovan then told the men to throw away the canteens. Later, when the weather turned dark and misty, the canteens were sorely missed.

The lieutenant colonel chose the Third Battalion, the Shamrock, as his attack battalion. The Shamrock's front-line companies soon got into trouble. Company I led off, followed by M. As the men followed the sunken road and moved toward the wire, Company I arrived first, followed by M in support. When the wire stopped I, M did not keep the proper length behind and bunched I. Enemy gunners could see this mass. The Americans sought to move out of the road, only to confront fire everywhere. Lieutenant R. B. DeLacour lost half his platoon in this bunching at the wire. German artillery knocked out two of his machine guns. With artillery fire from the north and enfilade fire from the east, DeLacour's men had "no protection whatever except along the sunken road, and we could not even attempt to send our wounded to the rear." Everywhere the enemy was triumphant, including in the air, where no American planes appeared. At 4:00 p.m., DeLacour saw five German planes circle over and bomb the troops, meanwhile reporting the regiment's position to the artillery in the Bois des Hazois.[3] The only resort of the companies was for men to crawl into shell holes, firing at what they could, as the hours elapsed toward nightfall, with troops behind them similarly in holes.

Setting an example for his regiment, Donovan went up with the support companies. Almost immediately beyond the trees beside the brook, the advance became disconcerting. Donovan had not calculated on the fire from Châtillon, taking for granted that in the three hours the division had allotted the Eighty-fourth Brigade to take the hill, the regiments of MacArthur would have accomplished that task. As the gunfire erupted he turned to Major Thomas J. Reilly. "Where the hell is that coming from?" he asked. The major told him laconically, "Why, that is from the Côte de Châtillon, of course." The Châtillon fire was intentionally aimed low, for men hit in the feet then would be hit in the head when they went down. The lieutenant colonel remembered thinking that he was just like a tenderfoot out in the

American West, because "those damn Germans" were shooting at his feet. At that juncture he said to Reilly, "We're worse off here than we would be if we moved forward."[4] He ordered the advance. The men went forward, convincing themselves the fire would be less the higher they went.

A remarkable account of the attack of the battalion and of the general ordeal of the 165th on October 14 appeared immediately after the war, written by Corporal Martin J. Hogan. He testified to what it was like to be in the front line on that awful occasion, carrying out (he did not say this) the theory of General Summerall that a divisional attack by all four regiments could find the weak part in the line. Hogan's book, beautifully written, probably edited, for it was published by the New York firm of Appleton, relates, "The fighting reached its highest possible point about eleven o'clock that morning, and hung at this point all day." Hogan or his editors were given to exaggeration and set out how every man fought his own battle against the enemy, the Shamrock fighters turning their ferocity against the foe in every manner possible. What the book did not provide in detail was supplied by the similarly published—in 1919—memoir of Chaplain Duffy, who described similar scenes. Hogan was wonderfully explicit in describing how he was clipped in the hand by a sniper. About 12:30 he was leading his men (whether a squad or a platoon is unclear) in an advance into a clearing, ten or fifteen paces in the lead, and just before he reached a shelter hole he saw a sniper in a tree, catching the glint of the barrel through the leaves. Warning the men behind him, Hogan slipped into the hole. The sniper still could see him and opened fire. Hogan took aim with his rifle at a deeper shade of dark in the tree. At that point a shot rang out and the sniper hit the knuckle of Hogan's left hand as he held the rifle. Several more shots rang out, and Hogan could not fire in response. He managed to run and crawl, in succession, back to a machine gun crew, fifteen yards to the rear. The gunners turned their gun on the tree Hogan pointed out for them, and the sniper tumbled down like a ripe fruit.[5]

When night came Donovan decided to stay with the men, for fear that if he left it would appear he had deserted them. He instructed company commanders to get their wounded out while night made it possible, which the commanders did. To Captain Henry A. Bootz he proposed a night attack, when the machine guns and artillery of the enemy would be blind save for what flares could reveal. Bootz years later told the American Battle Monuments Commission what happened to that proposal. Under General Pershing, retired beginning in 1924, the commission undertook to look into all the actions of the AEF and set out in detail what actually happened, so as to reveal lessons for future fighting, if necessary. Bootz wrote in 1930 that after the First Battalion relieved the Third early on the evening of October 14, Donovan asked him about an attack, and Bootz recommended attack by Companies C and A, with C, the company he commanded, on the right and B and D in support. Donovan gave Bootz command of the line. The enemy remained silent until the men reached the wire, whereupon a "terrific" machine gun and artillery fire opened and flares turned night into day. The infantry again could not penetrate the wire. "This is a good illustration," the former captain wrote, "to show that infantry alone cannot fight material [matériel]." He told Donovan, reporting to the lieutenant colonel in his shell hole, that he had so many replacements in his company they bunched up at night. He said that earlier that summer, when the Forty-second had attacked at Croix Rouge Farm and along the Ourcq River as the Germans retreated after the last attack of their offensive in 1918, he might have handled a night attack, but not on October 14 with all the untrained recruits.[6]

General Summerall, taking over V Corps, told General Menoher to get his artillery into action against the Kriemhilde Stellung, destroying the wire— and it was the wire, protected to be sure by machine guns and artillery, that tied down the Americans. Could it have been insufficient use of artillery that made the wire impassable? The men in the 165th New York had the ineradicable belief that their own artillery had not supported them. All the regiments of the Forty-second felt that way. But the 165th felt more strongly than the others because General MacArthur had taken the bulk of the Forty-second's artillery to reduce Châtillon, leaving the 165th with the 150th Indiana Artillery Regiment of the Forty-second's artillery brigade, possessed of 155s, not the 75s the men needed, or so they believed. Because of its heavy guns, difficult to move, the 150th Indiana was well behind the lines, not visible to the infantry. The heavy guns fired less frequently and, the men believed, less effectively. The men of the 150th themselves later explained that they fired blindly, "by the map," for they were without airplane direction, guessing the location of the German wire and where enemy artillery had secreted itself in the Bois des Hazois.[7]

Whatever the problems for the 150th Indiana, it is doubtful whether even if that regiment had been supplemented by the artillery brigade's two regiments of 75s there would have been much additional support for the 165th New York Infantry. Summerall desired the artillery to concentrate on targets fairly close together, putting all the guns on them at once, then shifting the concentration to other places in need of support—an attractive idea. When General MacArthur asked for and received the 75s he left only the long-range guns, and that meant no concentration. But the Indiana guns also had to support the other regiment in Lenihan's brigade, the 165th Ohio Infantry. That made them responsible for a line that extended more than four miles, far too long for any sort of heavy fire. Actually the rolling barrage that accompanied the 165th New York was so light the Germans believed it no artillery barrage at all but a concentration of American mortars.

A question could be raised, and the men of the 165th raised it, of why they were under fire not merely from ahead but also from the right, from Châtillon. The Eighty-fourth Brigade had taken the lion's share of the division's artillery, and also had the guns of the First Division, retained in line by the Forty-second when it replaced the First Division. The Eighty-fourth Brigade had not merely two artillery brigades but the 219th French Artillery with nine batteries of 75s, and a heavy French battery of eight-inch howitzers, together with two groups (six batteries) of French 105s and another group (three batteries) of 155s.

Another problem in artillery support for the 165th New York Regiment was the slow rate of fire of all American artillery, wherever located. The 75s of the Forty-second Division fired at one hundred shots an hour, the 155s at half that rate. The rate was absurd in support of troops in such a fix as those of the 165th, which needed all the support they could get. The 75 mm gun had a top rate of thirty shots a minute. The First Division attacking on October 4 fired its 75s at ten shots per minute. On September 29 one of the batteries in the Thirty-fifth Division's artillery brigade, when the battery commander believed, wrongly, that his division was in extremis (it had been so earlier but by the time the commander became active had gained protection of First Army guns that saved the division from German attack), pushed his rate of fire up to twenty shots. Increases could have been made for the Forty-second's 155s.

Even if the artillery had sent far more shells into the wire, as the men desired, it already had become known—and it was surprising that General Summerall, an artilleryman, did not know it—that enemy wire in 1918 could not be cut by artillery. On April 25 of that year, Colonel George E. Leach of the Minnesota light artillery regiment, the 151st, had conferred with General Lenihan about artillery support for a trench raid and had explained to the

Eighty-third Brigade commander that he would send five hundred shells into twenty feet of wire to see what they might accomplish. Leach evidently told Lenihan that German wire was handled differently in 1918 than earlier in the war. At the outset the custom had been to stretch wire between stakes. Later the Germans set it loosely, with play in the wire, so that when shells struck there was no result other than small breaks. Leach was keeping a diary and recorded that his test was a failure.[8]

An alternative might have been mortar fire. Albert M. Ettinger was a member of one of three mortar sections in the headquarters company of the 165th Infantry. There were four mortars to a section, each requiring three men to fire. Only one section went forward with the regiment, the others held in reserve for relief or to use in event of a German counterattack. Twenty men were taken from one of the infantry companies and used to supplement the twelve ammunition carriers of the mortar group of three sections, each carrier using a satchel that had two shells. Donovan told the section to send a barrage of shells into the wire to see the effect. "My God," the mortar man recalled, "I don't know how many hundred shells we sent into that wire." They had good effect in small areas, but the territory of the wire was too large, and Donovan called off the mortars.[9]

There was talk of using Bangalore torpedoes against the wire, but nothing came of it. These "exaggerated skyrockets" at the ends of long sticks, as the military historian Frederick Palmer described them, could be thrust into obstacles such as fields of wire and exploded like so many shell bursts. The colonel of the Forty-second's engineer regiment, J. Monroe Johnson, was adamantly against them and predicted they would be "absolutely ineffective." After a series of mishaps in attempting to prepare them, perhaps not altogether assisted by Colonel Johnson, the Forty-second gave them up.[10]

General Lenihan on October 15 brought up tanks to flatten the wire. For several reasons, as the 165th discovered, this did not work.[11] Wire cutters were taken forward, but Palmer related that they had not been improved since Cuba and South Africa twenty years before. The engineers and the 165th's infantrymen tried to use them, with light machine gunners and rifle grenadiers at their sides to protect them, to no avail. The effort was a waste of time and a waste of men, for the 117th Engineer Regiment lost seven men in supporting the 165th, which lost many more men. In a description in his book, Father Duffy related that bodies of the wire cutters hung on the wire until the end of the month, two weeks and more after October 14, when the

Second Division moved forward to replace the Forty-second and took St. Georges and Landres et St. Georges. The bodies mostly would have been men of the 165th New York.[12]

In the summer of 1918, Major General Beaumont Buck sponsored a device invented by his Third Division engineers that appeared, superficially, to hold possibilities of surmounting wire. General Pershing was interested enough to require all his divisions to send representatives to a trial at which the engineers showed off their device. It consisted of two widths of chicken wire, one atop the other, with the ends attached to poles, so that when confronted with wire infantrymen could put one pole on the ground and throw the other, wire attached, over the top. This could be done in a few minutes, whereupon infantry would walk over the chicken wire, each man pushing the wire deeper into the enemy's wire. The Forty-second's representative did not return with a report of enthusiasm. It seemed obvious that a single upraised enemy machine gun could kill each infantryman as he came over.[13] Too, the sponsor of the device was Buck, whose reputation in the AEF was diminishing, so much so that this ebullient Mississippian was relieved not long after the opening of the Meuse-Argonne, a victim of General Pershing's frequent way to dispose of unlikely generals, which was to send them home to, as the phrase had it, train troops.

The truth was that nothing was available to cut or mash or surmount the wire. The best course for wire was the same as for machine guns, which was avoidance. Toward the end of the war, tactics against machine guns became effective, and they were available in the AEF's fourth general attack that opened on November 1. But nothing in 1917–1918 availed for wire.

The cost for the 165th New York Infantry in going up against the series of obstacles that prevented it from taking its objective on October 14–15, 1918, was high: during its time in line, from October 12 to November 1, with the great bulk of casualties on the first two days of action, the regiment lost 195 men killed, 66 who later died of wounds, and 915 wounded.[14]

The other regiment in the Eighty-third Brigade, the 166th Ohio, enjoyed an altogether different experience from that of the 165th New York. This was due partly to the nature of its sector, to the left of the New Yorkers, and also one suspects—there is no direct evidence—partly to the personality of its colonel, Hough. The 166th was to fill the sector between the 165th and the Eighty-second Division. It confronted the smaller of the two villages within the German line above the brigade, the village of St. Georges. It did not have Châtillon on its right flank. It did have Hough as its colonel. The Ohio regiment had stood proudly for years as the state's National Guard force. Hough was a lawyer from Delaware, Ohio, just north of Columbus, and after the war became a member of the state supreme court, then federal attorney for the southern district of the state, then federal judge. He was a tall, bulky man who must have been impressive in a courtroom. His men adored him, evident in a story on the first two pages of the Kriemhilde Stellung chapter in the regimental history. The account was of a weary group of men, part of a regimental train, consigned to walking their horses and mules with all that meant for becoming mired in Meuse-Argonne mud. A wagon was stuck, and as the group was pushing they saw a burly figure standing at the side. A man said what they all were thinking, telling the "big stiff" to put his shoulder to the wheel. Hough did so. His words were, "Let's go, all together!" After which, with the wagon free, the men gasped as he got on a horse and rode off. "My Lord, that was the Old Man," were the words of the man who had called for help.[15]

The 166th under Colonel Hough did what it was required to do, which was to keep in line with the advance of the 165th New York. When the 165th stopped at the wire, the 166th stopped as well, happily without the enemy fire that greeted the 165th. One has the feeling that Hough, with his Ohio legal wisdom, knowing not to be rash, saw his fellow regiment getting into trouble and determined that the Ohioans would not do the same. An episode not long thereafter, in which he confronted Menoher and said what he thought, would seem to confirm this.[16]

2

While throughout the first day of fighting, Monday, October 14, the 165th New York was taking ever more casualties in a frontal attack against the Kriemhilde Stellung, the Eighty-fourth Brigade's two regiments, like Hough's 166th Ohio, were following a different course.

In MacArthur's brigade, the action essentially was under the command not of the commanding general but of Major Ross, who commanded the attack battalion of the 168th Iowa Regiment, which was the First Battalion. Ross, a National Guard officer from Red Oak, would command the Iowa Guard brigade in the 1920s, its reorganized form as a division in the 1930s, and then receive the lieutenant generalship conferred upon some Guard officers after retirement from active Guard service. Within the 168th Iowa in 1918 he was an easy choice for front-line command, akin to that of Lieutenant Colonel Donovan for the 165th New York. The commanding officer of the Iowa regiment, Lieutenant Colonel Tinley (promoted to colonel on October 18), was not a forceful officer and during the fighting of October 14–16 remained well behind in his command post at Hill 263, within the Bois de Romagne, where he received and sent on to brigade headquarters whatever messages the regiment's advanced P.C., advanced post of command, sent back to him. As General MacArthur told Tinley at the outset of the fighting, Major Ross was the key to the entire situation.[17] The Iowa regiment was much more active, because of the defenses surrounding the Côte de Châtillon, than was its fellow regiment in the brigade, the 167th Alabama.

The 168th Iowa was the right-hand regiment of the Forty-second Division, and its position requires a short account. Its center was Hill 263, within the Romagne woods. Replacing the Twenty-sixth Regiment of the First Division, it had not known its definite sector, and the Forty-second Division was mistaken in defining it, the combination of ignorance requiring investigation on October 13, which led to the deaths of three scouts and the capture of their leader, Sergeant Fleming. A further confusion was the sudden withdrawal of the 127th Regiment of the Thirty-second Division, which bordered the Iowans on their right; the 127th without notifying the 168th moved a kilometer to the east, and the gap had to be filled by a movement of Ross's First Battalion.

Forty-second Division headquarters, all its officers in their G system, in particular the G-2, Lieutenant Colonel Judah, was less than helpful in telling Colonel Tinley, and thereby Major Ross, the peculiar problem of the Thirty-second Division, which was the Côte Dame Marie. As mentioned, this was no simple hill, occupied by the Germans, but two hills, on the ends of a crescent-shaped ridge that faced into the line of advance of the Thirty-second. To make the capture of the ridge more difficult, it was a perfect site of observation, where German officers with field glasses could see the Americans of the Thirty-second advancing over a virtual plain, with only clumps of bushes and trees as shelter. The ridge, with its hills on the tips, Hill 258 on the right, Hill 286 on the left, was a major hill, almost as difficult as Châtillon to the northwest. Especially was this true of the right tip, Hill 258, where machine guns protected the defenders against attack from the plain to the south. In addition, the hill was a virtual cliff that would require scaling by attacking troops, not allowing for any simple advance. Prior to October 14 the regiments of the Thirty-second had done their best against 258, without result. It was necessary to take 258 before doing anything with the left hill, 286.

The difficulty of Côte Dame Marie was largely unknown to Ross's men, for all they could see was that German machine gun fire was coming into their sector from Hill 286. Lieutenant William R. Witherell in a later letter to the Battle Monuments Commission inveighed against the Thirty-second Division, blaming its commanders for failing to take 286 until late on the afternoon of October 14. He failed to comprehend that the Thirty-second actually took 258 earlier in a heroic action by seven men, under an adventuresome captain, who scaled the cliff and with rifle grenades killed the machine gunners at the top, forcing surrender of the survivors. This allowed their division to follow up, and the 127th Regiment, which Witherell sharply criticized as a laggard, unimaginative unit, to take 286.[18]

Witherell said that the Thirty-second lagged, and that was true enough, and with good reason, for the 168th received enfilade fire from 286 until late in the afternoon of October 14. An explanation of the circumstances, which could and should have been known to Colonel Judah and the commander of the Forty-second, General Menoher, would not have resolved the problem of the fire sooner, but would have made it easier to tolerate.

The problem of Hill 286 was increased by enemy fortification of a ridge that ran northwest to Hill 288; the defenders put machine guns along the ridge, making a line against the Iowans, with machine guns firing into their sector. Fire reached Major Ross's advanced post of command (P.C.), a makeshift place, a caved-in shaft, into the side of which his men dug a shelf for the P.C.'s telephone equipment. Trees had grown around the edges of the shaft. The hole protected its residents from the enemy machine guns firing over it, but it did not protect the runners who were coming and going, the only recourse for communication when the telephone line was out.

In addition, beginning on October 13 and lasting through the night until 8:00 a.m. on October 14, the men of the 168th were confronted by the fire of a group of eight-inch artillery pieces under French command, to the southeast of the Iowans. The guns, supposedly under Forty-second Division control, fired short, and men of the 168th Iowa were wounded by the shrapnel. In any advance to the north they had to contemplate not merely the German fire from Hill 286 but also the French fire, which Major Ross sought all night to stop, in order to advance to the ridge to the north containing Hill 288. The latter hill was the focus of Ross's energies during October 14, and the French guns could have done no better work than shooting up the hill.

In the early 1930s, Major Ross wrote long descriptions of what he did during the days of attack. On October 14, when he was to attack at 5:30 a.m. according to the division plan of battle, he did not move his battalion, the First, because of fire from the enemy along the ridge beginning with Hill 258 and going for two kilometers, more than a mile, northwest to Hill 288. He had been instructed to attack but could not because of the enfilade, also because of the shorts being sent over by the French unit. According to the division order he had three hours to move north, take Hill 288, take the smaller Hill 242 above it, take the two farms along the Côte de Châtillon, and occupy, together with the brigade's other regiment, the 167th Alabama, the entire Côte de Châtillon. The impossibility of the assignment, even if his men were walking, without opposition, as the Iowa regimental history described it, made him hesitant to move.

At last, at 8:00 a.m., General MacArthur telephoned Ross to advance, despite uncertainty that the French guns had raised their fire. Apparently by chance they raised it at the same time Ross received the order.[19]

By 10:15 Ross's men were on part of the ridge to the right of Hill 288, but it was 1:00 p.m. before the First Battalion had control of 288, including a trench on its north side. In preparing for an attack—for the hill was part of the Kriemhilde Stellung—the defenders had placed the trench forty feet down from the crest, in knowledge that it could not be touched by American artillery (likewise the Americans, so long as they stayed below the crest on the south side, could not be reached by German guns from the north). This shrewd placement of the trench added hours to the October 14 attack.

After capturing 288, the First Battalion needed reorganization. Companies C and D had done the work thus far, and Ross passed A and B through their lines. Meanwhile, he asked for Company H of the Second Battalion, which Captain Haynes, its commander, sent up. H put a platoon to work going down the ridge toward 286, mopping up machine guns as it moved along. Everything still depended on the Thirty-second Division, which did not get around to 286 until 4:00 p.m.

Lieutenant Bly of Company A came forward with his scouts and headquarters group to reconnoiter his place in the line and picked up sixteen prisoners. While they were being questioned at First Battalion headquarters, enemy artillery on the north slope of 288 fired upon and wounded some of the prisoners. From information gained from them, Ross arranged for the mopping up of the north slope below the trench, which by that time had been captured, and for the securing of Hill 242, between 288 and Tuilerie Farm on the northeast face of Châtillon. Company B on the left made advances, but A on the right did not, finding strong points wired. It was getting dark, and the decision was taken to cease operations until morning. Ross withdrew A and B to shelter behind 288, to await morning, when A could make a wide encirclement and take 242.

At dusk on October 14, Colonel Langdon of the 127th, Thirty-second Division, came to Ross's P.C. with information that the division had taken both hills of the Côte Dame Marie and in the morning would come abreast of the 168th Iowa, ending the enfilade fire.

As the morning of the fourteenth passed into afternoon, General MacArthur sent a series of communications to the Forty-second Division headquarters. As one reads the messages many years later, the Eighty-fourth Brigade's commander seems to have been explaining why his brigade, which according to the division order was to have cleared the enemy from everything between the top of the Bois de Romagne and the top of Châtillon in three hours, had not done so. MacArthur had put his trust in Major Ross, a wise decision, but evidently was uncertain how Ross would proceed. The front-line commander waited as long as he could (5:30 to 8:00 a.m.) and then needed hours to get up the south side of 288, more to take the trench on the north side, more to send men to eliminate machine guns along the ridge, all the while waiting for the 127th Regiment to take 286. Messages meanwhile passed from the Eighty-fourth Brigade's advanced P.C., a kilometer behind Ross's P.C., to MacArthur's P.C. near Exermont, three miles back of the fighting, thence to General Menoher at division headquarters. The messages bore evidence of excuse making.

The first message of importance was at 9:30 a.m., an hour after, according to the division order, Ross should have been at the top of Châtillon. It was a telephone message, from the Eighty-fourth Brigade to the Forty-second Division chief of staff, Colonel William N. Hughes:

> Major Ross reports at 8:30 a.m. he received information from the commanding officer of the 127th Infantry that the 127th Infantry was stopped south of Hill 286 and that it would dig in. This leaves Major Ross's right flank and rear exposed to heavy machine gun fire which it

has been receiving since the H hour and definitely impedes the taking of Hill 288 by Major Ross from the south or west. Can you not cause the 32nd Division to advance on Hill 286 and relieve this fire from the rear and flank? If Major Ross is not able to advance to the attack of the second objective H hour plus three hours now in progress I shall be forced to throw in my support battalion of the 168th between Hill 286 . . . [wires out by shell fire].[20]

At noon there came a field message from General MacArthur:

Have taken Hill 288. The fighting has been of the most desperate character. The battalion which took the hill is very badly shattered and I am making replacements. The position was splendidly entrenched, heavily wired and strongly manned. It had to be taken inch by inch in the most sanguinary fighting. It was superbly defended and heroically won.

The awkwardness of this message was that it went out a half hour before Ross's men took the trench on the north side, and they did not take the ground below until the next morning.

In early afternoon another field message was sent from the Eighty-fourth Brigade:

The following situation on my front at 2:00 p.m. The 32nd Division has not progressed a foot and the enemy still holds Hill 286. Along my right as I go forward I have to establish a line of defense against heavy German fire—artillery, machine gun, and infantry. . . . Along the Côte de Châtillon the enemy's position is reported by the 167th Infantry to be of great strength. It comprises a series of trenches with dugouts and new wire with steel posts. It is very strongly manned by both machine guns and infantry. One estimate puts the number of machine guns at 200. It is impossible, in my opinion, to take this position without a careful artillery preparation. My axis of attack, due to my exposed flank, is now northeast, and if I advance my line will be divergent from that of the 83rd Brigade. Is it desired that I should endeavor to proceed further?

After the war, the U.S. Army arranged with the German government for American officers to study German military records to obtain the German point of view of the actions of 1917–1918. This was a fortunate opportunity that would not be repeated after World War II, since the German Army's records from that war were largely destroyed by an Allied air raid. The officers studied the records of the German Forty-first Division, which opposed the U.S. Forty-second. The records showed that on October 13, 1918, the Forty-first had six heavy machine guns and seven lights on Châtillon. It is true that men from another division came into the area above Châtillon early on October 14; there is no record of how many machine guns they brought in.[21]

When the Forty-second Division replaced the First, the 167th Alabama Regiment replaced the First's Eighteenth Infantry Regiment, and its sector was without the confusion that affected the relief of the First's Twenty-eighth Regiment by the 168th Iowa. The Alabamians discovered themselves in the Bois de Romagne close to Hill 263. With the Iowans to the east, the 167th Alabama took the woods to the west, left of the Iowans, and moved north along the northwest side of Châtillon. The Côte de Châtillon, it will be remembered, was a triangle on a tip. On October 14 the 167th moved its line as close to the fortified edge of Châtillon as it could, close to the wire, and there it stopped.

The commander of the 167th was Lieutenant Colonel Walter E. Bare, taking the place of Colonel William P. Screws, who had become ill while the regiment was waiting to relieve the First; Bare commanded through the three days of attacks. One of his officers, Captain S. A. Wells, who was adjutant of the regiment's Second Battalion, wrote the Battle Monuments Commission in 1926 that the 167th attacked on neither October 14 nor October 15. Bare in his account in the division history said an attack opened at 8:30 a.m. on the first day and ended at 9:40 when the top of the regimental line along the northwest face of Châtillon had moved as close as it could to the German wire. He said he called off the attack "because I realized early in the advance that it would be futile to attempt to take the Côte de Châtillon by frontal attack and therefore I stopped the advance and held our objective."[22]

In communicating with General Menoher about the Eighty-fourth Brigade, there was not much that General MacArthur could say about his left-hand regiment, the 167th. He sent no messages about its accomplishments.[23]

Three

★ ★

OCTOBER 15

The task for the Forty-second Division on Tuesday, October 15, was to move forward with both brigades. As on the previous day, the Eighty-third Brigade under General Lenihan took the brunt of the fighting, with the 165th New York Regiment trying once again to get through the wire before Landres et St. Georges. On the right of the division sector the Eighty-fourth under Brigadier General MacArthur continued to move toward the Côte de Châtillon, if only by inches, as MacArthur described the movement of the 168th Iowa Regiment under Major Ross.

As during the initial day of action, the command situation again was a two-tiered arrangement, with little connection between the orders of the generals, on the corps, division, and brigade levels, and the men in line who were under control of local commanders, on the left Lieutenant Colonel Donovan, on the right Major Ross. The local leaders understood the obstacles, and their work was to devise solutions. The men saw these commanders and heard their orders.

On the left of the division line the 165th New York Regiment continued its attacks against the German line without any of the prudence shown by the other three regiments, until at 9:30 a.m. on October 15 a machine gun bullet felled Lieutenant Colonel Donovan. The bullet went through the bone of his leg and hence made it impossible for him to stand, let alone walk. He lay for five hours in a shell hole just below the front of the 165th's line, up against the German wire. He directed the regiment's fight, such as it could be against the wire and the rifles, machine guns, and artillery. In this condition if not somewhat before—on this latter score he never testified—he came to the realization that men against matériel was hopeless work; that such an attack could not be managed, let alone commanded; that if the contest continued a debacle was the only possible result. At around 10:30 that morning he gave the word to the front-line battalion commander, Major John Kelly, whose First Battalion had replaced the Third, that it was time to withdraw. This left everything to the slow but sure, as time would tell, movements of Major Ross in General MacArthur's brigade. Interesting, however, was the fact that the Eighty-fourth Brigade very nearly went off in a different direction by command of its young brigadier, who on the afternoon of the day before, October 14, had something else in mind.

1

Donovan had spent all night in a shell hole before Landres, so as to be with his regiment's attack battalion, which by October 15 was the First under Kelly, and on that day, a Tuesday, the attack opened again, at 7:30. Hope lay this time not in Irish capability but in the appearance of tanks, ordered up by Lenihan. Officers from brigade headquarters were scouring the roads for them.

Donovan meanwhile cheered Kelly's men with his presence, passing among them and telling them "we had to go through and that they were the fellows to do it."[1] The artillery barrage ran its course, and the First went forward without tanks. When the men started, Donovan went with them. Company C was on the right, with A on the left, closely followed by Company B on the left at a distance of three hundred yards. Company D was in reserve. At that moment the tanks appeared in Sommerance and came into line.

Upon reaching the wire the men dug in and waited for the tanks. Then the tanks that had gotten up that far—twenty-five started, sixteen arrived, ten went into action—turned around and went back. The seven-ton light Renaults were subject to mechanical failure. They were vulnerable to artillery because of their slow speed, five miles per hour. They were lightly armored, and machine gun bullets could penetrate them. Their drivers and gunners were easy casualties; one of the tank men was hit in the eye. German antitank guns, virtual squirrel rifles with three times the bore of rifles, fired from tripods, could put them out of action. General Lenihan said afterward that the tanks were useless. In that judgment he may have underestimated the importance of their failure, for once the tanks had raised the men's hopes of getting into the wire, their retreat let down the men's spirits. Donovan certainly was demoralized by it. Just as he was hit, he saw the tanks going back. He was told that one of them had gotten into the wire, but because he was on the other side of a slight fold in the ground his vision was limited.

With the failure of the tanks the lieutenant colonel asked for artillery fire, and his request was promptly complied with, "but the fire was not heavy enough to keep Germans down and give our men a chance to break through." To make matters worse, the enemy about this time began gathering a force for a counterattack from just south of Landres. Fortunately, the regimental trench mortars had been brought up during the night and opened on the Germans as soon as the First's men saw them. The mortars were in the north edge of the trees and brush above the brook where the Third Battalion and now Kelly's men had been before going up to the wire.

When the mortars opened there was an act of heroism by Sergeant Fitzsimmons. The gunners had the protection of sloping ground and could not see if their aiming was on target. Fitzsimmons ran forward to the top of the slope, "making himself an easy cockshot for the German gunners while he signaled to his men his corrections on their aim." He escaped being shot "by a miracle," the regimental operations officer, Captain Van Santvoord Merle-Smith, told the division historian, "and had the satisfaction of seeing the shells drop right among the gathering enemy, doing dreadful execution."

The attempted counterattack convinced Donovan that Kelly's battalion was too far forward, inviting attempts to cut it off. Kelly's force at the same time was suffering from artillery fire from the Bois des Hazois and from the Côte de Châtillon. "I therefore sent word for him to retire." Major Kelly had as many Irish tendencies as did Lieutenant Colonel Donovan and refused to accept an order to bring his men back until he had it in writing. Donovan in his shell hole complied, writing out an order.

It was just as Donovan summoned a runner to take up the written order that Major A. E. Anderson reached Donovan. Anderson had the reserve battalion—with the Third and First shot to pieces, his Second was the only one left. Captain Fecheimer came up with him and remembered saying to himself, about the lieutenant colonel, "How in hell is anybody going to get him out of here?" Anderson and Fecheimer lay down on the ground because of the heavy fire, and Donovan said "hello" and then, as bullets and shrapnel hit near the newcomers, said to Anderson, "You'd better get in here with me." To the captain he said, "Fecheimer, you get over in that foxhole over there." Fecheimer looked at the foxhole and saw two men in it, so he looked for another and saw one just behind the one the colonel had pointed out. He got in it, and shortly afterward a shell landed in the one with the two men, blowing them both to pieces. One, the captain remembered, was O'Connor from E Company, and the other was the regimental color sergeant, William G. Sheahan.

In the afternoon Donovan was carried back in a blanket to the regimental dressing station. Duffy saw him on arrival. The lieutenant colonel looked up from the stretcher and said, smiling, "Father, you're a disappointed man. You expected to have the pleasure of burying me over here." Duffy responded, "I certainly did, Bill, and you are a lucky dog to be off with nothing more than that leg in the shell hole." Donovan still believed, Duffy remembered, that with proper artillery protection and coordination of infantry the 165th could have gotten through.

Anderson took over from Donovan, and Captain Bootz took over the Second Battalion, which moved up to the line. The First at that point consisted of six officers and four hundred men, less than half its authorized strength. Anderson's battalion, now Bootz's, established a line by the brook, a small but workable reverse slope, hence protected from artillery fire. This became the 165th's line until October 24, when the 166th Ohio took over. On the night of October 31–November 1 the Second Division replaced the Forty-second, just before First Army opened the Meuse-Argonne's last attack.

The failure of the 165th before the wire was followed by a devastating analysis by the corps commander, General Summerall, and not merely an analysis but relief of the Eighty-third Brigade's commanding general, Lenihan, as well as the regiment's commanding officer, Colonel Mitchell, together with Merle-Smith and the regimental adjutant, Lieutenant Harold J. Betty. On October 15, at 6:25 p.m., the division commander, General Menoher, called Lenihan and ordered him to bring Colonel Mitchell and the regimental staff to the divisional headquarters at 7:00. The request seemed unusual, and the Sixty-third Brigade's commander must have been uneasy about it, but not long after 6:25 Summerall appeared in Lenihan's P.C., canceling Menoher's plans for the 7:00 meeting. Merle-Smith, a New York City lawyer, a 1911 graduate of Princeton University who in the 1920s would become an assistant secretary of state, was accustomed to courtroom procedures and easily sensed what the corps commander was about. After a few questions to Lenihan and Mitchell, who asked Merle-Smith and Betty (the latter had been in the front line with Donovan) to describe what happened, the inevitable followed: the relief of everyone present.[2]

The obvious question is who was running the Forty-second Division? Summerall did not even employ the courtesy of having Menoher present. Without reference to him, he handled the matter himself.

Summerall's position appeared in a letter from Menoher to Summerall, a mere formality, perhaps dictated by the corps commander, dated October 17. In a preliminary the letter said Lenihan always had been considered an excellent officer. The German defenses on October 14–15 were very strong but were considered possible to breach. Lenihan, however, and his fellow officers, lacked the necessary "push," and for that reason they were relieved. Summerall's endorsement followed, carrying the same date as the letter, which was forwarded to the new First Army commander, Liggett. The mission of the 165th, the assault on the German position, was "extremely important to the operations of the corps." Lenihan had shown no dissatisfaction with his regimental commanders, the colonels of the 165th New York and 166th Ohio, and did not think "that there was any lack of leadership." Summerall did not think the brigade or regimental commanders had visited the troops. In no case, he said, did it appear that the assault troops reached the wire, or that casualties had occurred in or beyond the wire. Many casualties had occurred and without commensurate advantage. Summerall said Colonel Mitchell had delegated an explanation of what happened to two staff officers and he felt that Mitchell and the staff were "mentally defeated."

Chaplain Duffy was not present but quite evidently heard Lenihan's explanations and those of his officers and later wrote that the brigade commander, his close friend, was not a good man to explain something to an irate corps commander. An Old Army officer, the brigade commander gathered his forces and requested another hearing, sending a letter through channels together with supporting letters. Duffy wrote one of them, perhaps not a wise thing to do considering the military points of the occasion.[3] The general's letter might well have been written by Duffy and Merle-Smith. Lenihan stood by his regimental commanders, he said. They had performed well on previous occasions, and he felt there had been no deterioration of their ability. The brigade commander had visited his regiments. "I have without exception made it my habit to make personally a reconnaissance of the terrain occupied by my command, and to go among the troops prior to any new undertaking. During action, as soon as it is possible to do so, without losing touch with the brigade and the supporting troops and artillery, it is my custom to go right forward to the leading battalion." He visited the support battalion prior to the attack and found the men in their usual fine spirits. (He did not say he saw the attack battalion.) He said the problem was machine guns and artillery on the right, meaning the Eighty-fourth Brigade's sector, where the Eighty-fourth had not taken the Côte de Châtillon when the Eighty-third attacked. Lenihan came as close as he could to laying the blame on MacArthur. "While it is evident that machine gun and artillery fire from the front had something to do with stopping the attack, the primary cause of the failure was machine gun and artillery fire from the right flank."

In defense of Lenihan, Merle-Smith said that the following message, in substance, had gone to Donovan: "We will surely attack tomorrow morning, the honor of the regiment, division and the American Army rests on the success of the next assault. You must carry along the rest of the regiments of the division. Inspire the old Irish fighting spirit in every man. Go to it, old man, it's up to you."

By and large the judgment of Duffy about the meeting of the officers with Summerall was repeated in the statements of Lenihan and the others a few days later. These gave the advantage to Summerall, whose comments tended to dominate the contentions. The brigade commander and his officers resorted to details rather than the larger picture as drawn by the corps commander. They of course were under the strain of deferring to a general whom they disliked—*detested* would not be too strong a word. They had to meet assertions with explanations, difficult to do without seeming to deal with smaller issues. Colonel Mitchell spent several hours at the front on October 13 and also two days later on the fifteenth. Like Lenihan he had absolute confidence in Donovan and hence remained at his P.C. on October 14. He wanted to keep in touch with the brigade commanders. The day preceding the attack he held a conference with his field officers and impressed on them the importance of carrying out the mission "no matter how difficult it might appear." He satisfied himself that each officer thoroughly understood what he said. "I am sure there was never any question in the minds of the regiment relative to our being able to reach our objective."

The appeal for reconsideration brought the V Corps inspector, Colonel S. Field Dallam, into the issue, an embarrassing position for Dallam, who had to report to an irate senior officer. He did not help himself by changing his mind. In his first appraisal he described the Eighty-third Brigade as possessed of "excellent fighting qualities." The Eighty-fourth Brigade, had it been able, would have taken the Côte de Châtillon, "which exposed the right flank of the Eighty-third Brigade." He admitted the lack of visibility in the Eighty-third's sector. Menoher had reported the mopping up of the Côte de Châtillon, which confused Lenihan. The wounding of Lieutenant Colonel Donovan may have confused Donovan into ordering a withdrawal. Monitoring all of this, Dallam approved the action of Menoher in removing Lenihan. Reconsidering, he pointed his finger at MacArthur's brigade: "the Eighty-fourth Brigade did not capture the Côte de Châtillon until October 16th. This exposed the right front and right flank of the Eighty-third Brigade to severe enfilade fire."

Summerall refused to accept Dallam's second finding, in an endorsement to General Liggett. The latter told Lenihan he would find another brigade for him, and sent him to the Seventy-seventh Division, momentarily out of the line but soon back in. A colonel was commanding Lenihan's new brigade, and the Seventy-seventh's commanding general allowed the colonel to remain in command during the following days, which kept Lenihan from active command until the end of the war.

Lenihan retired a major general. His memoir, "I Remember—I Remember," compiled many years later by his wife, Mina, from tapes her husband made, does not mention his relief by Summerall.

A few words are in order about a brush, if one might so describe it, between General Menoher and Colonel Hough of the 166th Ohio Regiment. Summerall had remarked Lenihan's satisfaction with the colonels of both the 165th and the 166th, implying that they both had been delinquent. Evidently he said this to Menoher and probably asked the Forty-second's commander to warn Hough. The 166th had kept up with the 165th, although when the latter went up to the wire and a few yards, perhaps, beyond, it was ahead of the division's other regiments, including Hough's. The Ohio colonel, a Guard officer, and as mentioned an important legal figure in Columbus, would not push his men beyond that. He protected his "Ohio boys." Their casualties from October 12 to November 1 were 52 men killed, 41 dead from wounds, and 437 wounded.[4] In regard to clothing and overcoats and blankets he saw to it that they had them as soon as possible; on October

18 his regiment's supply trucks brought up the winter uniforms and winter underwear and overcoats and blankets. Menoher later took a swipe at Hough by describing him as the best housekeeper in the division.[5] He would not say that Hough was the best fighting colonel. But words could not move Hough. He was not to be bluffed. He had been in many courtrooms. In the regimental history, published in 1924, it is clear that the author, a former 166th Guard captain, talked to Hough, who said that Menoher had called him in on October 17, stated the corps commander's views, and commented on what he called the "low morale of the 166th." Hough took issue with the two major generals, saying the judgment was unfair, that "no one man can take fatigue out of men who have been living in water filled holes in the ground with no overcoats and but one blanket, seeing their comrades killed by shell fire or dying from pneumonia. The men want action. If you hold me responsible for the condition which you allege to be true, then remove me now." The writer added that without doubt this plain statement and fearless championing of the men prevented "any further meddling with Colonel Hough's position."[6]

2

By 10:30 a.m. on October 15, the second day of fighting by the 165th, it was clear that the New York regiment was not going to do any more fighting against wire, rifles, machine guns, and artillery. It had been the only regiment possessed of the old Irish fighting spirit. Hough's regiment, the 166th, would not even move against the wire. It also was clear that the Eighty-fourth Brigade, MacArthur's men, would do whatever it had to do but do it slowly, with the fewest possible casualties.

In the 168th the front-line commander, Ross, was determined to move as rapidly toward Châtillon as he could but avoid all rash behavior.[7] He put his own battalion, the First, on the line initially and then on the night of October 14–15 brought in Company H of the Second Battalion to reach out on the right to the 127th Regiment of the Thirty-second. On the morning of October 15 his four companies of the First Battalion finished up the taking of the north slope of Hill 288, routing the Germans out of whatever defenses they had there, including the trench part of the way down from the summit, together with shell holes defended by machine guns. Proceeding north he tended, with due care, to the defenses of Hill 242, the German smaller position above 288.

In the taking of Hill 242, Companies A, B, and D formed the attack, from right to left, with C in support. Ross's technique was to work his companies around both sides of the hill. Passing it, Company A moved to the west and attacked Tuilerie Farm, capturing machine guns, but in the face of heavy fire moved back to the reverse slope of Hill 288. There it met the other companies, which had moved back because the brigade artillery was going to shell the places to the north, which it did for forty-five minutes. The companies moved up again, attacking at 3:00 p.m. Company B flanked Tuilerie from the east and took all the buildings but the barn, remaining there until after dark, when it moved back to the northern slope of Hill 242. Meanwhile, Company F of the Second Battalion had been moved into support, meaning that Ross now had his own four companies plus half of the Second Battalion.

During the advances, Ross's men behaved in exemplary fashion. These were American infantrymen at their best, an inspiring group. When Company D suffered from the direct fire of two Maxims on a side hill across a valley, Lieutenant Spalding called Sergeant Maynard Nelson to him and said, "There's a couple of Boche machine guns out there—think we'll have to get them." "Think we will, Lieutenant," said the sergeant. "How many men shall I take?"[8] Ross moved among the troops and afterward described the kind of men he had. He was following Company B to the west of the Bois de Romagne, everything quiet and the movement progressing as in a drill. He called to one of his runners to go to Company C and tell Lieutenant Witherell to push faster out of the woods. The runner—he did not remember his name—started off to deliver the message. In a minute or two the major heard German machine guns open all along the base of the Côte de Châtillon, together with a mortar from the direction of Tuilerie Farm. Just a short time later he turned around, and there was his runner with blood dripping from both hands. A burst of machine gun fire had caught him, and he had come back to tell the major he had not been able to deliver the message.[9]

That night, October 15–16, Ross's men took Tuilerie Farm. At 8:15 a brigade officer, Lieutenant Wright, sent MacArthur a message that Ross said he had a platoon in Tuilerie and was trying to get in more men.[10] Musarde Farm at the bottom tip of Châtillon had been taken that afternoon by the 167th Alabama Regiment, establishing the regiments along the approaches to Châtillon.

Lieutenant Witherell of Company C of the 168th spent the night of October 15–16 in a shell hole twenty yards behind a hedge separating his men from the German line. Ross, the front-line commander, did little better, scooping out a good-sized shell hole over which, a luxury, he rigged a tarpaulin. It was to no avail; in the middle of the night the rain collapsed the hole. The major sank into mud to his armpits. A fellow officer dug him out, and for the rest of the night the two men, soaked to the skin, walked around to keep from chilling.[11]

All the while a solution was being worked out for taking the Côte de Châtillon the next day, October 16, in the time announced by the V Corps commander but without the horrendous casualties acceptable to Summerall. His subordinate, General MacArthur, had a curious part in the solution, but nothing like the part he described to Major General Charles D. Rhodes, that is, that he led the troops by example.

To understand the solution at Châtillon, especially why it came from the 167th's officers, requires a departure from the fighting of October 14–16, back to an action late in July by the 167th Regiment in the Aisne-Marne offensive following the battle of Soissons. In this engagement the regiment attacked and took the Croix Rouge Farm, just before going on to attack German positions before and across the Ourcq River. Both actions, Croix Rouge and the Ourcq, were extremely costly. It will suffice to describe what happened at Croix Rouge, memory of which lay at the front of the thoughts of the 167th's officers who recommended the solution to the Côte de Châtillon.

In the days after the failure of the last great German attack in the series of five attacks during the spring and early summer of 1918, the exuberance of leaders of the French Army was understandable, for it became clear that the Germans were capable of being defeated. This exuberance showed itself in the belief that the cavalry divisions that both the French and British maintained might be used, a scenario that enthralled officers who in their minds' eyes saw thousands of horsemen riding with lances lowered, pursuing the foe helplessly fleeing on foot. In those heady days of late July, when the German Army was withdrawing back of a series of rivers, the Ourcq being one, for the purpose of shortening the line, General Jean Degoutte, commander of the French Sixth Army, in which the nascent American I Corps was represented in part by the Forty-second Division, sent word through General Liggett, who passed the order to General Menoher, to attack a German rearguard unit, the Fourth Guard Division, troops of which held Croix Rouge Farm. To push out the defenders the Americans were to attack with a bayonet charge.

The order of Degoutte, duly transmitted, went to the 167th Alabama Regiment, which on the afternoon of July 26 followed it out to the letter, and the result was a minor chapter of the war's history but no minor chapter in the history of the 167th. The regiment undertook reconnaissance of the farm and sent word to the brigade and presumably the division and corps that the Germans were in force in Croix Rouge. The commander of the 167th, Colonel Screws, protested any action to a point that, as he described it, he was on the verge of losing his command.[12] With no support from corps and division, MacArthur's predecessor with the Eighty-fourth Brigade, Brigadier General Robert A. Brown (West Point, a member of the class of 1885), was forced to call his officers together and tell them to make the charge. Brown's order to the artillery to fire a preparation and barrage did not get to the artillery, and there was no protection. The result was a melee. The two battalions that went into Croix Rouge Farm suffered 50 percent casualties. Lieutenant Colonel Bare wrote that "our men were literally mowed down by traversing machine gun fire.... The ground was literally covered with killed and wounded, both American and German. For some distance you could actually walk on dead men." When the fight was over it required almost all the remaining men of the battalions to carry the wounded back two and one-half miles to the division dressing station. A burial party the next day interred 283 bayoneted men of the Fourth Guards, but this was cold comfort for the 167th's casualties.[13]

MacArthur, the division chief of staff, not close to what happened, saw Croix Rouge as a great romantic action. He remembered the gallantry: the men took the farm "in a manner which for its gallantry I do not believe has been surpassed in military history." He saw one of the occasions in the war when the bayonet was decisive. "It was one more occasion which proves the fallacy of trying to judge the bayonet by the number of bayonet wounds found in the hospitals. This, for the reason that practically all of those bayoneted died where they fell."[14] Observers of later AEF actions such as Captain W. Kerr Rainsford, the historian of the 307th Regiment, Seventy-seventh Division, wrote of the uselessness of the bayonet, and MacArthur probably was referring to them. The captain said that in hospitals no one ever saw a bayonet wound, that wartime posters of Americans stabbing protesting Germans were artistic concoctions, offered for public imagination, and that such an event never happened in the Meuse-Argonne. This was true, it did not. It did happen earlier, at Croix Rouge, and General MacArthur remembered the gallantry.[15]

Lieutenant Colonel Bare testified that Croix Rouge was no inspiring engagement, and so did the 167th's surviving officers and men. Bare went around the farm afterward and saw how the Germans placed twenty-seven machine guns in lines and marked aiming points in front, on trees, at which gunners could fire so that bullets would strike the oncoming Americans. Bare wrote that above the brigade level there had been a near complete lack of thinking about the attack.[16]

This was not the end of bayonet talk, as the I Corps divisions immediately thereafter approached the Ourcq River. About midnight on July 26, Colonel Blanton Winship from I Corps arrived at the 165th New York with orders for a general attack across the Ourcq, the regiment to make the assault that night without using rifles, "but . . . to confine themselves to the bayonet." The regimental commander of the time, Colonel Frank R. McCoy, said that Winship insisted, "Degoutte was determined to keep the Germans moving and that, if necessary, I must sacrifice my command in the effort." This bayonet order was rescinded when it was discovered that the enemy had disappeared from the front.[17]

Total casualties of the Forty-second for pursuit of the German Army from the Oise to the Aisne were 945 men killed in action, 269 died of wounds, and 4,315 wounded—a total of 5,529.

To return to the taking of the Côte de Châtillon, on the first day of the fighting, October 14, after a half-hearted attack by Lieutenant Colonel Bare's men against the northwest face of Châtillon that lasted an hour and a half, the 167th's front-line battalion called off the attempt to penetrate the wire. The fighting for the rest of that day, and for the next, the fifteenth, was on the side of the 168th Iowa Regiment. At 5:00 p.m. on October 14, or close to that time, General MacArthur, embarrassed by this pace, called General Menoher on the field telephone with a message of considerable import. "Lacking orders to the contrary," he said, "I will continue the attack during the night. I am pushing from the south with 168th Infantry and from the west with the 167th Infantry." Then followed a proposal: "I will give orders to do no firing but to clean up with the bayonet." He inquired, "Is it all right?" Menoher replied: "It is." MacArthur concluded, "All right, I will give those orders. Good night."[18] An order to attack with the bayonet, no firing allowed, went out at once.

The response of Major Ross to the bayonet order was straightforward. He explained that the 168th could not move as the order required. "As it was impossible to move to the north in the general direction of la Tuilerie Farm to Côte de Châtillon on account of the wire and mass of machine gun fire directly on our front, and a flank movement to the left in order to clear and evade the machine gun fire and the wire would have later on caused intermingling of our battalion and that of the 167th in the darkness, the regimental advanced P.C. was advised of the situation."[19]

The 167th had no dispositions that prevented carrying out the order, but the latter, when it came down to battalions and companies, produced an uproar. Who started it is unclear; it could have been Lieutenant Royal Little, commanding Company E of the Third Battalion. E was one of the two companies of the 167th in the line against the northwest face of German defenses surrounding Châtillon. The lieutenant had come to his company as a replacement; he was not a member of the Alabama Guard. He appears to have possessed a considerable background. He certainly wrote the best of all the detailed descriptions when responding to the Battle Monuments Commission, a several-page double-spaced typewritten memoir; he intended it as such, he told the commission officer handling his correspondence. His stationery read, "Special Yarns Corporation," address South Boston. Little was nothing if not blunt about the order concerning an attack that night with the bayonet. He was "amazed," he wrote, "to receive a hastily written order that Company E with another company in support was to make a night attack immediately, penetrating the enemy wire and driving the Germans northward 'at the point of the bayonet without firing a shot.'" His company was to occupy the entire Côte de Châtillon, defended by probably more than five hundred of the enemy. "The order was so utterly ridiculous that I immediately rushed to battalion headquarters to find out who had perpetrated this abortion."[20]

Little's battalion commander, Major Ravee Norris, had the same opinion about the bayonet order. The major had sent out patrols to cut the Châtillon wire, without success, even after reducing them from eight men to two or three. The wire remained untouched, though a number of men of his battalion sacrificed themselves in their endeavor to open the way. As at Croix Rouge, his efforts meant nothing to whoever sent out the bayonet order. "After dark the fourteenth, much to my surprise and consternation I got an order to assault the Côte de Châtillon with the bayonet! No firing allowed!" Norris's account in the division history has inaccuracies, including his description of what must have been an immediate meeting of some considerable satisfaction with Lieutenant Colonel Bare, who he relates told him orders were orders. Bare, undoubtedly with Croix Rouge Farm in mind, would have sympathized with Norris.[21]

There was a delay in the execution of the bayonet order, for General Menoher intervened, ordering artillery fire on Châtillon to see what it might do. At around 6:00 p.m., Company E and the other attack company in line for the Third Battalion (the commander of which also had protested to Major Norris), along with other units that might be caught in the artillery fire, withdrew to the Bois de Romagne. The fire by heavy guns seems not to have accomplished anything beyond postponing the bayonet charge. Lieutenant Little remembered that two of his men were killed and many injured during the night from shorts.

On October 15 the 167th did no fighting. General MacArthur could not begin the bayonet charge until nightfall, and nothing happened to alter the plan. Shortly after dark, the brigade commander summoned Lieutenant Colonel Bare; the lieutenant colonel of the 168th Iowa, Tinley; and the commander of the brigade machine gun battalion, Major Cooper D. Winn, to consider what to do. Hardly had the group begun to deliberate than a telephone call came through from the corps commander, who spoke so assertively into the field telephone that Bare heard what he said: the côte was the key to the entire situation, and he wanted it by 6:00 p.m. the next evening. MacArthur told Summerall, "We will take the Côte de Châtillon by tomorrow afternoon by six o'clock or report a casualty list of 6,000 dead. That will include me." The brigade was under full strength, and six thousand meant every man in it. According to Bare, after such an assertion to Summerall, MacArthur calmly proceeded with the meeting.[22] Unknown to the group, the corps commander had just relieved Lenihan and the three headquarters officers of the 165th.

The group came around to what Lieutenant Little in his letter of 1926 to the Battle Monuments Commission (and one must believe the same was true for all the officers of the 167th) had seen as the way out of their predicament and that of the generals. Little wrote that he thought the wire along the northwestern side of the côte was new, just strung, and had not been photographed by Air Service planes. American planes were not much in evidence during the Meuse-Argonne, in part because their commander, Brigadier General William Mitchell, was more interested in bombing than in reconnaissance, and also because during the entire battle there were only a few days without heavy cloud cover and rain. It happened, however, that the chief of staff of the Forty-second Division, Colonel Hughes, had obtained an aerial photograph showing a passage through the German wire to the right of

Musarde Farm, that is, on the northeastern face of Châtillon.[23] This presented a possibility.

There was another consideration, but it is unclear how much it affected the conversation that evening. Lieutenant Little, an acute observer, wrote that on the northeastern face of Châtillon there was no wire, only a row of machine guns. He assumed that the Germans in preparing the Kriemhilde Stellung had not gotten around to completing their line on the northeast.

For whatever reason or reasons, it became clear to the conferees that any attack should be on the side of the 168th where the defenses were less formidable. The authorship of the idea is not clear. Norris said it was his, having told Bare before the meeting. Bare also took credit. It was not that of General MacArthur, who took credit later.

In the discussion, Major Winn of the machine gun battalion may have had much to do with the result.[24] The proposal advanced by Lieutenant Colonel Bare included a machine gun fusillade that would drive enemy machine gunners into their dugouts. Winn described the idea as a machine gunner's dream, giving his battalion a chance to show what it could do. He had been aghast at the manner in which the First Division, before the Forty-second relieved it, distributed its machine gunners to the smaller infantry units, breaking up the First's battalions and even its companies, to Winn's opinion so fragmenting them that they were ineffective because their mission, to replace any lack of supporting artillery, was lost sight of by small-unit commanders. In replacing the First he inquired of an opposite, one of the First's machine gun battalion commanders, where the guns were, and the commander did not know, could not tell him. Winn had kept his battalion under his own control. In the relief, he placed Companies B and D in the Petit Bois and had with him at Exermont the battalion train and Companies A and C. He desired to bring them to Hill 263 and fire a protective barrage to get the German gunners away from their guns.

Bare told the group he had a plan that would be successful, but that he would have to encroach on Colonel Tinley's territory. General MacArthur asked him to outline the plan. The 168th Iowa was on the right of the 167th Alabama, and Bare described a deep ravine between Hill 263 and the sector of the 168th. He told MacArthur that he could move a battalion into the sector, using the ravine, with overhead machine gun fire keeping enemy gunners down until, without observation, his troops could reach the northeast face of Châtillon. Upon hearing this explanation Colonel Tinley spoke up and said, "I will be delighted not only to cooperate in every way I can but will take orders if necessary from Colonel Bare." Bare wrote that Major Winn spoke strongly in favor of this idea, involving his battalion. General MacArthur, Bare said, acquiesced. General MacArthur warned Colonel Bare about one particular, namely, that he was not to mix the 167th with the 168th, for this would confuse the regiments.

The 167th's commander went back to his regiment, telephoning ahead for all of his battalion commanders to meet him at his headquarters in, as he put it, "a hole in the ground." There they laid their plans. Bare relieved Major Norris from his battalion so that he could watch over the development, Norris wrote, of the entire plan from the 167th's side. The Third Battalion, under Major George A. Glenn, was to go around through the ravine. That night Glenn delegated command to a first-rate man, Captain Thomas A. Fallaw. The captain had been a sergeant on the Mexican border in 1916, when National Guard units protected border towns from raids by General Pancho Villa while General Pershing's Punitive Expedition sought to destroy Villa's ragtag force. When the Forty-second went to France he became an officer. On the night of October 15–16 he gathered what he believed he needed, an enlarged platoon of one hundred men, drawing on 167th men in the Bois de Romagne available for the foray into Châtillon.

Four

★ ★

OCTOBER 16

What happened at the Côte de Châtillon on Wednesday, October 16, was a fine example of what two National Guard regiments could do in World War I, 1917–1918, which was to break through the German main line. This the regiments did very much on their own, without supervision from the generals who supposedly supervised their movements. The regimental officers—Major Ross on the side of the 168th Iowa, and Lieutenant Colonel Bare on the side of the 167th Alabama, with assistance from Major Winn of the brigade machine gun battalion—and their men did the work.

The German Army was a formidable foe and even in late 1918, near the end of the war, had a great deal of fight left in it. True enough, its strength had been dissipated in the five attacks that constituted the German general offensive in 1918 between the months of March and July. Thereafter the enemy shortened its lines, retreating from salients, going back to what was described as the Hindenburg Line, named after its titular commander, Field Marshal Paul von Hindenburg (the quartermaster general, Erich Ludendorff, was the German Army's commander). The new German position consisted of three lines, named after Wagnerian witches, Giselher, Kriemhilde, and Freya. The first, the Germans yielded to the Americans in the initial days of the Meuse-Argonne. The second, the Kriemhilde, they chose not to yield, to hold in every place, and this was where the Forty-second Division found itself on October 14–16. The reasons for holding the Kriemhilde related in part to the terrain above the line. Below it the terrain was difficult, filled with ravines and ridges and trees and scrub difficult to get through, everything dominated by hills from which observers could see the Americans coming. The land of France above the Kriemhilde became much easier, for it was undulating, almost inviting, and untouched by war; the Germans had occupied it in 1914. Too, in September–October 1918, they had no time to prepare the third line, the Freya, which was more a plan than a reality. If the Americans broke through the Kriemhilde, there would be no time at all to make the next line defensible; the German Army would have to retire again, this time to the other side of the Meuse, and it was uncertain if the river itself could be held against the enemy from the New World.

A point could be made that General Pershing's generals, the commanders of corps, divisions, and brigades, made too much of the Kriemhilde Stellung, exaggerating its importance. This probably was true, although they could not see that truth at the time. Pershing was a good organizer of the AEF, but tactically he was not good. He had expended the fighting ability of First Army by battering at the enemy—on September 26, October 4, and again, it seemed, on October 14—with the Forty-second Division's 165th New York Regiment being a prime example. He did not realize what the First Army was capable of, if properly managed. When, on the day the regiments of the Eighty-fourth Brigade attacked Châtillon, General Liggett took over First Army, he at once declared what became two weeks of careful reorganization, bringing everything together, reclothing and feeding the front-line troops, bringing up supplies, bringing up the heavy artillery and massing heavy guns, and light ones as well, in preparation for the attack on November 1, 1918, that went through to the Meuse and beyond. In that sense it was not necessary for the 168th and 167th regiments to take Châtillon, for the army could have swept over the place two weeks later. But this was unknown on October 16.

1

As during the previous two days, on the sixteenth the fighting on the front of the Eighty-fourth Brigade again appeared to be mostly on the brigade's right side, the sector of the 168th Iowa Regiment. Everything started out that way. There the cautious Major Ross was in control; his senior, Lieutenant Colonel Tinley, was little more than titular commander of the regiment. By the morning of October 16, Ross was using his own battalion, the First, and had taken two companies from the Second. He would take the other two. Before the day was over he also had the Third Battalion, with Tinley in charge of little more than the regimental P.C.

The geography over which the 168th would have to go can be thought of as a sort of wheel, with the axle at Hill 288, now entirely in the hands of the regiment. From Hill 263 in the Bois de Romagne, 288 was perhaps half a mile, something less than one kilometer. From 288 north to Musarde Farm, and also to Tuilerie Farm, was a half mile, the routes forming spokes from the axle at 288. Distances hence were not great, although if one was walking and attempting to avoid hostile artillery fire they were magnified, if the walkers moved, as they should have, in a zigzag fashion.

If one thought of distances as spokes in a wheel, then Châtillon was something else, the triangle balanced on one tip. Just below it lay Musarde Farm, with Tuilerie higher up the northeastern side, all in the sector of the 167th and 168th. The stretch of open meadow rose to the last ridge south of Châtillon. Over the crest of the ridge was a hedge, and beyond the ground dipped and rose again to the woods that fronted the côte. The woods virtually covered Châtillon's southern slope and reached to the right within a hundred yards of Tuilerie Farm.

The task of Major Winn's machine gun battalion was to create such a hail of bullets that gunners serving enemy machine guns lining the northeastern face of the côte would take to their bunkers and stay there while the 167th Infantry's contingent under Captain Fallaw got into the swale and followed it until the men found a way to go north into Châtillon. Meanwhile, on the 168th's side, to the right, the Iowa regiment too could get into the woods lining the côte and go north toward the top of the hill.

For the task of forcing enemy troops under cover, Major Winn was nothing if not ingenious. He said afterward that his guns enfiladed every trench in Châtillon.[1] He placed them on the forward slope of Hill 263, a half mile from Châtillon but close enough for easy coverage. Each gun had a skeleton crew, enough to fire it. He protected the crews as well as possible from shrapnel by digging in and improvising other cover. He put all his companies in position and brought in every gun they possessed, including spare guns. The total in action was sixty guns. During the forty-five minutes of the barrage he claimed to have fired nearly a million rounds, which figure seems impossible, for a machine gun cannot fire all the time and usually does its firing in bursts. He told his gunners to fire as long as the guns did not overheat.

The barrage appears to have worked, for Winn pointed out proudly that casualties in the 168th Regiment and in the 167th were relatively few. He may have been correct in this, that his fusillade was a good deal better than artillery. The latter, especially the 75s, suffered from flat trajectories, limiting their targets. Machine gunners could better calculate their fire, and at a long range the gunners knew how high to raise the guns to allow rounds to drop to their targets. Châtillon held the advantage of being a hill, with almost any target within range.

Winn's pride in what his massed guns did was vindicated, perhaps, by the use of a machine gun barrage two weeks later when regiments of the Eighty-ninth Division prepared to advance in the attack of November 1. One of the colonels remarked the entire suitability of the guns, despite the strangeness of having bullets whistling above the heads of his infantry and the strangeness of the sound, like a million or more angrily buzzing bees.[2]

At 10:30 on October 16 the First Battalion of the 168th moved into the swale before the côte. The companies, right to left, were F, H (which had become available after the Thirty-second Division took the two hills on Côte Dame Marie and was able to come up to the line of the 168th Iowa), C, and B. C succeeded in making a hole in the hostile machine gun defense, which the other companies widened by taking out German machine guns next to the original hole. The first progress was on the right and moved down to the left, toward Musarde Farm. F Company had two platoons in a charge when challenged by a machine gun on the left. H Company meanwhile rushed in and found a circular trench containing four guns. As gunners swiveled around to catch F, H came in behind and took the gunners.

One thing led to another. Seeing at a glance the fortuitous situation with the enemy guns, Lieutenants Miller and Witherell of C Company started their men across the swale. Going as fast as they could in the soggy ground with their equipment, and yelling at the tops of their lungs (like Comanches, the regimental history put it), to the purpose of scaring the defenders, they got across to the côte's woods. The lieutenants had only a detachment, twenty-odd men, and lost eight killed, but they got the others over.

The experiences of the men after making their ways into Châtillon varied, every man having a separate adventure. Witherell took a few men and passed through the woods into an open place, when they found themselves in front of a group of Germans. The lieutenant emptied his pistol at them, narrowly missed being knocked senseless by a rifle butt, and together with his detail retreated into the woods.[3]

It was at this time, with the friendly machine gun barrage still on—the men jumped off at 10:30, and the barrage ran for another fifteen minutes, firing into the reverse slope of the côte, over the crest—that Corporal Joseph Pruette performed one of the most exemplary acts of that day in the Meuse-Argonne before the Côte de Châtillon. Major Ross, following the troops, came on Pruette, an Iowa schoolteacher, dancing on top of a German dugout and shouting, "I've got 'em! I've got 'em!" His face was streaked with sweat and he was holding two German potato-masher grenades, one in each hand; he had picked them up on the way. As the regimental history described the wonderful scene, he indeed had 'em.[4] From the entrances to the dugout came piteous cries of "Kamerad!" The men inside were fearing that Pruette would throw a grenade into their midst. As he shouted "Come out! Come out!" they filed out, Lieutenant Witherell having persuaded him to spare his prisoners. A German officer, seeing Pruette's corporal's stripes, said in broken English that he, the officer, would surrender to an American officer. "Cut out that noise or up you go in smoke!" shouted Pruette. Figures vary as to how many Germans surrendered, from sixty-four men and four officers, to sixty-eight men and four officers, to ninety-one men and two officers. Whatever, it was an achievement for which Pruette received the Distinguished Service Cross.

Ross and his men of the First Battalion, reinforced by two companies of the Second, went up beyond the woods at the bottom of Châtillon, into the open place leading to the top. But there they met with a large disappointment. Having almost gained the prize, the côte, they had to give it up. At around noon, forming a line near the crest, they discovered that the defenders had machine guns on a small hill numbered 260, and there seem to have been field guns involved. The 168th Iowa found its force, four companies, too small to hold its position. There was nothing to do but go back down Châtillon, to the foot of the côte above Musarde Farm.

The time was around noon, on October 16, and after the repulse Ross did the only thing he could. He had no idea where Captain Fallaw's force was and did not know if Fallaw's men had gotten through the machine guns along the northeastern face of Châtillon. He sent messages to the 167th and, as he described it, "demanded" that his fellow regiment get into the fight.[5]

Here, incidentally, was another example of what can happen to a tactical plan in an action. The fact was that any plan could go awry, whatever its merits. In fact, the plan for October 16 had not gone awry, but one aspect of it had to be scrapped. In his meeting with the regimental leaders, General MacArthur had insisted that the two regiments not mix, not undertake attacks together.[6] In the event, the next morning it was perfectly clear that the 168th Iowa was not strong enough to take on the German forces on the côte, that it would have to have help from the 167th.

When Ross sent his request, it turned out that the 167th already was in the process of making the rest of the plan work, but the two regiments had to work together. The 167th needed the morning to make its arrangements. Lieutenant Colonel Bare remembered that the force of Captain Fallaw started off at 6:10 a.m. and moved along the top of the Bois de Romagne, following the woods, which went along below the northeast face of Châtillon. Thereafter it was one attack after another.

For the work of Fallaw's men the best source is Lieutenant Little's account to the Battle Monuments Commission.[7] As commander of Company E at the bottom of the 167th's line next to the German wire, close to Musarde Farm at the tip of Châtillon, he was easily available for service with Fallaw, who chose him as his second in command. Little wrote his detailed description largely, he said, for his own benefit, bringing together his memories. His memoir has proved valuable indeed, as the Forty-second Division records for the entire action of October 14–16 are sparse, and especially the records of the 167th Regiment for October 16.

According to the lieutenant, after arriving below the côte in the 168th's sector, "We then advanced in one long skirmish line and moved forward until we reached the protection of the hedge running along the crest of the ridge in the field south of the Côte de Châtillon." At that point the force was just south of Musarde Farm, which itself lay south of the tip of Châtillon. From there to the edge of the woods to the northeastern side of the côte the ground sloped so that as soon as the force passed the hedge and moved into the draw before the woods that bordered Châtillon it was exposed to the German machine gunners—what numbers of those had not gone into their bunkers during Winn's machine gun fusillade. By this time, 10:30, the sixty machine guns of the major had raised the trajectory of the shots, allowing the men of the 168th and 167th to enter Châtillon.

Lieutenant Little, who was on the scene and wrote in detail, said there was no wire on the côte's northeastern face. He assumed that the Germans had not had time to finish Châtillon's defense line, as they had done on the northwestern face. This was a debatable point. Lieutenant Colonel Bare, generally reliable, described wire. The division chief of staff, Colonel Hughes, said he authorized aerial reconnaissance that resulted in photographs showing a path through the wire in the 168th Iowa's sector to the right of Musarde, a path that the Germans had used when defending the Bois de Romagne against the First Division some days earlier. Bare said that during the meeting with MacArthur on the evening of October 15 the general had produced a map showing a pathway through the wire.

The Little account says nothing of a passage but describes how the enemy machine gunners, seeing the Fallaw force go over the crest of the ridge in front of Châtillon past the hedge, opened fire and began to turn the force back. At that juncture, he said, the captain held a "council of war," presumably behind the ridge crest, which decided that at a given three blasts from Fallaw's whistle, repeated by anyone with a whistle, the men would charge, the entire line, against the machine guns, in hope that the Germans would be frightened by the sudden appearance of the entire group and abandon their guns. This was what happened, when the group was halfway through the swale, approaching the trees that fringed Châtillon.

The place where the men charged would have been between Musarde Farm and Tuilerie Farm, as the latter lay next to the northeast face of Châtillon. After the charging line got through to the fringe of trees along the face, with the machine gunners fleeing north, fearful for what sort of attack by the Americans they faced, Captain Fallaw reorganized his group for the pursuit.

To one man of the 167th Alabama, Major Norris, who had carried to Lieutenant Colonel Bare the objections of his two front-line company commanders to the bayonet charge, the three blasts of Fallaw's whistle and the echoing blasts by possessors of whistles in the Fallaw group were music to his ears.[8] Norris had been delegated to watch the 167th's plan in action and had gone around with Fallaw as an observer. He had barely cleared the machine gun line, with the defenders running toward the top of the hill, when a bullet caught him in the heel. He lay on the ground trying to judge by the sounds what was happening. As the yells of the men as they went up the hill became more faint, he knew they had not lost. The yelling and shouting produced German artillery fire; instead of bursting in his vicinity, the shells were well to the north, convincing him the men had succeeded. He was terribly anxious for the outcome, he wrote. Finally a sergeant came back and told him "we've got the hill, and a lot of these G—d d—ned Heinies as well." Norris laughed with relief "and also they tell me had tears in my eyes."

While this was going on, Lieutenant Little ran around to the northwestern side of the côte. He stopped at the regimental advance P.C. in the Bois de Romagne for authority and then organized a group of one hundred men from the units in the open space facing the northwestern side of Châtillon. Major Abner Flowers of the Second Battalion commanded this force, similar in size to the Fallaw force.

In knowledge that the defenders of Châtillon on the northwest side would be nervous about having Fallaw's troops at their rear, Flowers's men advanced into what had seemed an impenetrable face of the hill, and with great fortune they discovered a passage in the wire—not just into it but through it. The passage was similar to (and, Flowers would have thought, had been created for the same purpose as) the passage Colonel Hughes had discovered to the right of Musarde and that General MacArthur had shown on the map in the group meeting the night of October 15.

With the defenders distracted, the group of the 167th on the northwest face went through the wire and over the tank trap. The Germans, like those at the machine guns on the northeast face, fled north. Before proceeding in pursuit, the men of the 167th blocked off the trench so that enemy troops, attempting to filter back in, could not simply proceed down their own trench.

2

The Fallaw force from the 167th and Ross's 168th companies went up the Côte de Châtillon together at 1:00 p.m., and there were immediate signs of success. This time Ross had the support he asked for, although not from a large force. The 167th was in the process of getting another force through from the northwestern face of the côte. The Eighty-fourth Brigade observer at Ross's P.C. was quick to see the good signs and at 1:10 sent a field message: "Major Ross, in the face of strong machine gun resistance, is making progress through the woods up the slope of Côte de Châtillon."[9] General MacArthur, given what General Summerall had told him over the field telephone the previous night and his own somewhat, one could say, nonchalant reply, must have breathed a sigh of relief—the major gave promise of saving the situation, with assistance from the 167th. At 1:45 a message went out: "Lieutenant Wright reports that word has just reached him that the enemy is fleeing from the north edge of woods of Côte de Châtillon and that they have been brought under our artillery fire, several direct hits being made among which was one upon a caisson trying to escape. The line of the 167th runs about 500 yards within the woods of Côte de Châtillon and good progress is being made." At 3:45 another field message went out: "Major Ross is making good progress and has just about reached his objective."

These messages by no means showed what was going on, in particular the anxieties of Major Ross. The advance was slow work, and not very sure. In the early afternoon the commander of the 168th's Second Battalion, Captain Haynes, and his intelligence officer, Lieutenant Wallace, made a reconnaissance to the line and saw how tight everything was. The First Battalion and two companies of the Second were going forward but, as Haynes and his fellow officer saw, were facing what looked like the makings of a counterattack. The two returned to Ross's P.C., and the major at once asked for two more companies, E and G. Lieutenant Doolittle, Company E, was to filter his company in through the open space between Musarde Farm and Châtillon woods to shore up the left, and do so without calling attention to his movements so that the defenders of Châtillon, by this time concentrated at the very top of the côte, would not notice and respond with machine gun and artillery fire. Captain Younkin of Company G was to advance to the right and filter the men into the line in support of E, at the same time extending and protecting the open flank on that side.

Turning back the counterattack also required close work on the part of Fallaw's men from the 167th. A member of the regimental headquarters company, Sergeant Ralph Atkinson, managed to get a single mortar up Châtillon—it was all he had of the four assigned to headquarters. He looked up toward Hill 260 and saw what appeared to be two hundred or two hundred and fifty Germans, presumably some of them the men driven north by the Americans, organizing to come down on Fallaw's fairly small force, which was linked, but barely linked, to Major Ross's line of the 168th Iowa. A man of decision, the sergeant put his men to work with their rifles and submachine guns, saving out two men to help him with the mortar, for all the latter required was a three-man crew. Usually a man firing a mortar needed a carefully chosen place from which to fire, with solid ground as a base. Atkinson had no time and held the big mortar between his legs and fired. He sent Private John C. Austin up ahead to observe his shots and if necessary correct them. The first shot landed squarely in the midst of the enemy force and did dreadful execution, which Atkinson followed by shot after shot. Afterward, he felt that together his men and the Fallaw force had saved the day with the would-be counterattackers.[10]

At the time the companies of the Second Battalion of the 168th went into the line, and the men of the Fallaw group got up the hill, there still was concern that the Germans at the top were massing to come down, possibly to mount a counterattack. This was a standard tactic when units of the enemy lost ground, and the Americans knew to expect it. When Haynes and Wallace, wounded by shrapnel on their return, staggered into Ross's P.C. and told what they had seen, an artillery observer standing there said, "Let me fix it," and called in the coordinates to gunners of the Fifth Artillery Regiment, part of the First Division's artillery brigade that had been attached to the Forty-second Division. A few minutes later the guns opened with a roar and, like the assistance of Haynes's two companies and of Atkinson with the Fallaw group, helped break the counterattack.[11]

Fifteen minutes after the German counterattack failed, the 167th's force from the northwest face joined Fallaw. The two groups from the regiment went on up and drove the defenders from 260 and over the crest and down into Landres et St. Georges.

The enemy had fought with all the experience it had gained in previous engagements and until the end was ready to seize every advantage. A field message to MacArthur from the next day related how a patrol had gone out with twenty men from the northeast corner of Châtillon, into the woods two hundred yards toward the top of the hill near the crest, entering from the northeast, east, and center at the same time, and found a 77-mm field gun in the center of the woods. The gun had been freshly camouflaged with a supply of ammunition laid in.[12]

The nature of the fighting for the côte was fairly clear, in that some of it was downright bluffing by the 167th's groups on both sides of the northwest face of Châtillon. It certainly involved pursuit, which because of the bluffing was not as sanguinary as it could have been if the Germans had resisted all the way. Had the attempted counterattack at 3:00 succeeded, there would have been many casualties on the American side. Suffice to say that the total casualties for the Eighty-fourth Brigade, which of course included losses to the 168th Iowa from taking Hills 288 and 242 and Tuilerie Farm, and to the 167th from taking Musarde, were much smaller than those of the 165th New York up against the defenses of Landres et St. Georges. The 168th between October 12 and 19 lost 90 men killed, 53 dead of wounds, and 566 wounded; the 167th, 81 killed, 36 dead of wounds, and 554 wounded.[13]

Lieutenant Little thought afterward that both of the attacking forces of the 167th, in particular the Flowers group, had been too small, that it was a mistake not to have thrown in more troops. He may have been right, and if so that would have reduced casualties. On this score Flowers did not testify; he did not leave an explanation of why he took only a hundred men. He may have believed that the course of the developing action was too uncertain and that to take more might have jeopardized the 167th's line on the northwest face of Châtillon. He could not be sure the machine gunners on the step of the tank trench would give up and move to the north.

Major Ross, and on the side of the 167th Lieutenant Colonel Bare, had done their best to avoid casualties, employing no such tactics as those used on October 14 by the 165th New York Infantry. There were heroes in the Eighty-fourth Brigade, but they always avoided gallantry. They did seize their opportunities. Sergeant Atkinson received the Distinguished Service Cross for his act in the face of certain danger that had a large effect on taking Châtillon. Private Thomas C. Neibaur received the Congressional Medal of Honor for facing similar personal danger. A little fellow, and quite young, a replacement in the 167th from Idaho, he was an automatic rifleman and placed in a shell hole up front to repel the threatened counterattack. During a shelling he found the hole too small and moved to a larger one, only to find he had landed in a group of two dozen Germans. Before he could realize what had happened they jumped on him and took his submachine gun. This was in the midst of the fire that the Fifth Artillery Regiment laid down to eliminate the counterattack. When the fire became less dangerous the Germans decided to crawl back to their line, taking Neibaur with them. In the excitement they forgot to take their guns. Finding a new shell hole, they settled in. Neibaur drew his pistol—he also had a pistol that the Germans hadn't taken—and took over. Once clear of the hole he forced most of the Germans to accompany him back to the American line.[14]

It can be said that all the men killed, and all those wounded, were heroes. It was noticed by medics that the outset of being wounded was not as difficult as what followed, that there was a period of numbness in which the wounds seemed almost not present, unfelt. A medic in I Company, 168th, Lawrence O. Stewart, included a story in his book about a lieutenant colonel who lost an arm. Stewart admitted that he himself was not present at the scene, since the colonel was in a different unit. He claimed the wounded man was seen calmly removing his West Point class ring from the hand of his severed arm. The story illustrated the extent to which the numbness was present. Stewart was more convincing on another score, how it felt to be buried alive by a shell burst, because it had happened to him. "The next thing I knew, my head was looking around for the rest of me and couldn't find it. I wiggled my neck and it still seemed to be attached to something. Some earth gave way and as I shook myself hard I freed my hands and dug myself out of the ground, where the exploding shell had buried me up to my neck."[15]

When the fighting was all over on Châtillon, the 168th's Third Battalion replaced the First and Second. Company I relieved E and C companies. Just as the first detachment of E started for the rear a question arose as to whether Company I had relieved an outpost in the woods. Corporal Arthur F. Brandt, who had a habit of volunteering for disagreeable duties, stepped out and proposed to lead the relief. Enemy artillery was busy with whatever it could do to the Americans, and a hundred yards out a burst of shrapnel struck four of the party, including Brandt. When he was found, several minutes later, he was in agony, one side of his face shot away, unable to talk. He was wounded in the hip as well, and shrapnel had struck him other places. He was the only individual who knew the way back to the company, and upon being put on a stretcher he indicated by signs that he wanted to be placed at the front of the group so that he could direct the outpost men back. He took charge and directed the return trip through the woods, by this time almost totally dark. It was raining. Reaching Hill 242, the hill above 288 that had occupied the 168th Regiment on October 15, he found other wounded who needed to go back to the dressing station behind 288. No one knew the way, and Brandt led them. Then he collapsed, mission accomplished, and the next day died.[16]

Gas casualties were always present in actions involving the Forty-second Division in the Meuse-Argonne, as with all divisions in that horrible place. Gas accounted for 20 percent of casualties. It is true that many men were not properly diagnosed and may in fact have been malingerers. Others were recruits without gas training and uncertain of why they were so tired, and it may be that they were worn out by the constant rain and cold and lack of blankets and winter uniforms, as was in fair part the trouble in Colonel Hough's 166th Ohio Regiment. Whatever the actual causes, the reports of gas casualties were high and resulted in fewer men available for service at the front or in support of the fighting troops.[17]

However small the casualties, though in individual human cost they surely seemed large, Châtillon was a victory and worthy of celebration. The Forty-second Division's daily intelligence summary described what had happened.

> On the afternoon of October 16 the 84th Brigade by terrific and prolonged fighting against well organized and savage defense, succeeded in penetrating the Kriemhilde Stellung at its apex on the Côte de Châtillon which is said to be the strongest point between the Argonne and the Meuse. At this point there is a heavily wooded slope with strong wire. Here a large garrison with artillery support and the usual large supply of machine guns on which the enemy base their defense, offered grim battle and was driven back by the furious attacks of our infantry. We now hold Côte de Châtillon, and have organized the forward slope of the hill against possible counterattacks. Two enemy attacks to dislodge us during the afternoon were complete failures.[18]

The members of the Rainbow Division in 1917–1918 believed that their division was a fortunate part of the AEF, that Providence looked after them. For a while in the Meuse-Argonne there had been concern about their fortune in attacking the Côte de Châtillon. When the 167th reached the crest and drove the Germans into Landres, the regimental historian, William H. Amerine, took the occasion to celebrate what his regiment had done, and may have stretched his imagination. By the will of Providence, he wrote, a rainbow had appeared for the Forty-second Division as it entered every fight but one, that for possession of the Côte de Châtillon. The 167th's Third Battalion under Major Norris fought for two days close to the wire, October 14 and 15. Then on October 16, Lieutenant Colonel Bare sent the Fallaw force around to the 168th's side. The group of the Second Battalion under Major Flowers went up. The rainbow thereupon appeared, "flashed across the heavens."[19]

Côte de Châtillon, Meuse-Argonne, 1918. The mist was typical of October.
(111-Signal Corps 28382, National Archives, College Park, Maryland)

The commander in chief, General John J. Pershing. Major General Charles T. Menoher, commander of the Forty-second Division, opens his car door. (111-SC 16781)

Major General Charles P. Summerall, commanding V Corps. (111-SC 17200)

General Menoher. (111-SC 31841)

Colonel William N. Hughes, chief of staff, Forty-second Division. (111-SC 31843)

Lieutenant Colonel Noble B. Judah, chief of intelligence, G-2, Forty-second Division. (111-SC 31842)

Brigadier General Michael J. Lenihan listens to the commander in chief address a group about to be honored. (111-SC 23727)

Then Colonel Douglas MacArthur and General Menoher. (111-SC 5744)

Color guard of the 165th New York Infantry Regiment. *Left to right,* John Curtin, William Schmidt, William G. Sheahan, Herbert A. Schwartz. Sergeant Sheahan was killed on October 15, 1918, before Landres et St. Georges. (111-SC 23724)

Lieutenant Colonel William J. Donovan, front-line commander before Landres et St. Georges. (111-SC 25158)

Francis P. Duffy, chaplain of the 165th Infantry, before the grave of Quentin Roosevelt, son of former president Theodore Roosevelt, whose plane was shot down by German fliers. To Duffy's left is Colonel Frank R. McCoy, at that time commanding the 165th Infantry. (111-SC 18910)

Colonel Benson W. Hough, commanding the 166th Ohio Infantry Regiment,
standing on the lowest step, with his staff. To Hough's left is his aide, Captain
Robert S. Beightler, commanding general of the Thirty-seventh Division
during World War II. (111-SC 46297)

Left to right: Captain Glenn C. Haynes; Major Lloyd D. Ross, front-line commander of the 168th Iowa Infantry; Captain Charles J. Riley. (111-SC 46332)

Staff of the 167th Alabama Infantry. *Left to right:* Captain W. J. Cole; Lieutenant Colonel Walter E. Bare, acting regimental commander; Captain G. A. Glenn; Lieutenant Oscar Greshaw. (111-SC 23923)

Brigadier General Robert A. Brown and Lieutenant General de Boullon. General Brown was relieved and reduced in rank after the crossing of the Ourck. (111-SC 17103)

Brigadier General Henry J. Reilly, historian of the Forty-second Division. (111-SC 29671)

Colonel William P. Screws, commanding the 167th Alabama Infantry, ill at the time of the attack on Châtillon. (111-SC 7732)

General Pershing decorates General MacArthur, with General Menoher reading the citation. To MacArthur's right are the commander of the 151st Minnesota Artillery Regiment, Colonel George E. Leach, and Lieutenant Colonel Donovan. (111-SC 23728)

General MacArthur. (111-SC 18905)

General MacArthur. (111-SC 18904)

Five

★ ★

CONCLUSION

Any study of reputation must inquire about omissions and commissions, and in this regard the record of Brigadier General Douglas MacArthur in the taking of the Côte de Châtillon, October 14–16, 1918, contains two glaring miscalculations. One was his acceptance of a division order that depended on his brigade and could not possibly work. The other was his proposed bayonet charge at night, no firing allowed, which would have broken his two regiments and sent him to the general officers' depot at Blois, where the AEF disposed of its battlefield failures.

There was another aspect of the action at Châtillon that deserves attention, namely, that on the crucial days of fighting, October 14–16, General MacArthur does not appear to have done anything substantial by his two regiments, the 168th Iowa and the 167th Alabama. All decisions were in the hands of Major Ross and Lieutenant Colonel Bare and their subordinates.

Last, one must ask why General MacArthur over the many years that followed could not have said, at any of the many times when his praises for Châtillon were sung, that he, the brigade commander, depended entirely on his regiments, that their commanders were the key to the taking of Châtillon. One must ask why, instead, he told General Rhodes that there were two kinds of generals, the one mere administrators, the other leaders in the field, and that at Châtillon he led the troops by example.

When the division field order for the action of October 14–16 came out, it was clear that the preliminary move, the very base of the plan, was the attack of MacArthur's Eighty-fourth Brigade against the Côte de Châtillon beginning at 5:30 a.m., October 14. By 8:30, three hours later, the brigade was to have taken Châtillon, thereby making it possible for General Lenihan's Eighty-third Brigade, principally the 165th New York Regiment, to attack straight toward Landres et St. Georges, which was denominated as their third objective (the first was their jumping-off point, the second a line just before the German wire), and go on a mile or so to the north, the fourth objective and their stopping point. Everything rested on the Eighty-fourth Brigade's taking Châtillon on the action's first day, in three hours.

That this field order was dramatically silly, and could not possibly have worked, should have been evident to any commander in the field, but the fact was that it was not. General Summerall had only been in his new position, corps commander, for three days, and his support for the plan perhaps could have been excused for that reason. General Menoher was directly responsible, and it seems impossible that he could have sponsored such an order. General Lenihan met an inquiry by one of his colonels with silence; he was not about to testify on a division order that seemed not—although the ensuing action would instantly show otherwise—to involve his brigade. General MacArthur, whose men were required by the order to take a German position defended by enemy positions on Hills 288 and 242, and then to take two fortified groups of farm buildings, and after that to take the côte itself, defended by two rows of machine guns and on the northwest side by two rows of staked barbed wire and a sizable tank trap, might have gone to Menoher and said plainly that the order was impossible. He chose the course of Lenihan, even though the order directly depended on his troops performing a miracle. John H. Taber, the intelligent historian of the 168th Iowa Regiment, remarked that the men of MacArthur's regiments could not have walked the distance required in the time allotted, let alone fought their way through the most cunning series of barriers the German Army could have invented for protecting the Kriemhilde Stellung.

In the AEF's early months in the line, either in trench warfare or in the war of movement that opened with the great German offensive of March–July 1918, there might have been a feeling in some divisions that what the field order required was possible. It seems strange, however, that the Forty-second Division's leadership put out such an order in October, after its experiences in the Aisne-Marne offensive, at St. Mihiel, and in the Champagne, all actions of magnitude. One wonders even more how as intelligent an officer as Lieutenant Colonel Donovan could have asked, when the 165th started out and the machine guns and artillery from Châtillon opened their enfilading fire, where that fire was coming from.

One wonders, too, why Lenihan and the other commanders of the 165th Regiment did not make points about how they could not take their objectives while receiving fire from the côte. Instead, they were careful not to blame their fellow brigade, which had failed to take its objective and, so far as they could see, had done nothing at all in the three hours given it to attack.

If General Lenihan was blameworthy for refusing to give an opinion on the need of the Eighty-fourth for more time, so it seems that General MacArthur was blameworthy for not protesting a division order that was patently impossible to carry out. Lenihan was Old Army and, as were so many of those cautious officers, was careful not to trample on the work of superiors. MacArthur's career path had been different. He had served in the Philippines, to be sure, where the Regulars almost all had gone, but he had not suffered the years in small posts in the American West at a time, and here one speaks of the 1880s and 1890s, when larger circumstances seemed unlikely. He might have been more adventuresome than Lenihan, and yet in the event he was not. At that moment he was in an especially advantageous position. He had been promoted to brigadier general not within the division or the AEF but from Washington. At the time of his transfer to command of the Eighty-fourth Brigade he was under orders to return to the United States, to train a brigade of the newly organized Eleventh Division at Camp Meade, Maryland. This might have given him the confidence to go to Menoher, whom he knew well from having served as chief of staff during Menoher's entire service with the Forty-second, since November 1917, and say frankly that the division order for the action forthcoming had to be changed. Instead he was as cautious as Lenihan.

In considering why MacArthur did not protest the order, it is helpful to go back to the relief of General Brown on August 5. Here was a case where the brigade commander listened carefully to his officers and men and took their advice. He had the courage to stand up to General Menoher and his staff officers, the latter of whom he almost openly despised. The fifty-nine-page dossier on Brown's relief and reduction in rank is clear in showing his close-ness to the units he commanded. He was a shrewd commander, and his detailed description of the labors of his regiments beginning with Croix Rouge Farm is believable. He had control of the regiments and advanced them with tactics that brought out the best of what they were capable. That best became increasingly less as the days passed after July 26 and Croix Rouge, down to the brigade's last action under his command, the taking of Nesles on the other side of the Ourcq on August 4. His officers stood up for him in the most forthright manner when he told Menoher beginning with the Croix Rouge Farm affair that the men were increasingly tired and should not be shoved. Colonel Screws of the 167th Alabama, who was a forthright com-mander, supported Brown to the hilt. When the inspector general from AEF headquarters, Colonel M. G. Spinks, who not long afterward was promoted to brigadier general and had made up his mind about General Brown, sought to get Screws to say otherwise, that Brown was indecisive and had collapsed mentally and physically on the field of action, Screws stood firm:

Q. Did you think he had a good grasp of everything?

A. Absolutely.

Q. What was the condition of the men of your regiment—the physical condition about that time?

A. You mean which time?

Q. During this period July 25th to August 5th.

A. The physical condition of the men after we struck the Ourcq River, which was July 27th, our Brigade which had been in since we left La Porta in camions, we had been constantly on the go. . . .

Q. What was the state of their morale?

A. The morale I would say was excellent under the conditions. . . .

Q. Did you see General Brown display any more evidence of mental or physical fatigue than the other officers of the brigade?

A. Not in fact, he was up in the morning and around on the job and seemed to have the situation well in hand and was clear in all his orders.

Q. Were these matters discussed with General Brown or reported to him?

A. Yes; you mean the condition of the men?

Q. Yes.

A. Yes sir; I reported it to him and made a written report to him. I recommended verbally and in writing that the regiment be relieved due
to the tired condition of the officers and men. I think this was on July
31st.[1]

During the relief of General Brown there was no chance that General
MacArthur, as division chief of staff, would listen to the side of the general
and his regimental commanders. He was a team player. He took his judg-
ments from division headquarters, which was the safe side on which to be.
The division staff members were against Brown, to a man. MacArthur
accused Brown of mental and physical collapse and helped send him into
oblivion as a Regular officer; the demotion would blight what few years
Brown had left in the Regular Army.

The experience of seeing what happened to Brown, who said things as
they were, one must presume made an impression on General MacArthur,
who was silent when he received an order that made no sense. There is not
much more one can say, except for the obvious. If he did not understand
what the division attack order for October 14, Field Order 36, meant for the
Eighty-third Brigade—Lenihan's defeat—MacArthur was incompetent in
the field. If he did understand and was protecting his career, he was no leader
of men, leading by example.

The bayonet order similarly may have been a career-protecting move.
Here the danger was from the corps commander, Summerall. The commander of the Eighty-fourth Brigade perhaps needed to do something dra-
matic, not yet evidenced by the stentorian order of the next night to take
Châtillon. Summerall had a habit of advancing his ideas as if there were no
alternatives. He had done the same thing on July 18 when he just made commanding general of the First Division and, not knowing the terrain or the
obstacles facing his regiments, nor, especially, the ineptitude of throwing
men against matériel, which was what was happening in the attack of the
moment against the Germans in the Soissons salient, he threw them in.
Colonel Conrad S. Babcock, one of his regimental commanders, refused to
push his men after the regiment took 50 percent casualties, and Summerall
forced him out of the division. Babcock, a Regular, with friends in AEF headquarters, went to the Eighty-ninth Division, where he performed brilliantly;
unlike General Brown, he had a second chance against a system of command

often based on ignorance. He hated Summerall for the rest of his life and, during World War II, when he wished to go back into the army and instead was permanently retired, wrote a detailed memoir testifying to what happened.[2] Nonetheless, Summerall did have admirable qualities. He understood the use of artillery when most AEF commanders did not. When he commanded a division there were no loose ends—after he controlled it long enough, which required months, to know his officers and men. MacArthur may have sensed a need to do something, after failing to protest the division order that required his brigade to do something it could not.

The bayonet order may also have been the result of impulsiveness—a snap decision, not thought out. To be sure, if taken by itself it is not possible to see how it could have been thought out.

The order was delayed by, of all things, an order from Menoher, equally of no value, to put artillery fire on Châtillon that night, October 14. Then, to the fortune of everyone, Lieutenant Colonel Bare made the suggestion, essentially an argument, that part of his regiment move into the 168th Iowa's sector.

As for General MacArthur's absence from any of the decisions that counted at Châtillon, that is undeniable. It could be argued that, after all, he presided over the decision on the evening of October 15 to put a force from the 167th into the sector of the 168th, the decision advanced by Bare and agreed to by Lieutenant Colonel Tinley and Major Winn. This indeed was a decision, except that it was not General MacArthur's. He acquiesced in it. Afterward, as has been remarked, there was a question as to whether this was the decision, the plan it might be said, of Bare or of Major Norris. Lieutenant Little wrote in 1926 to the Battle Monuments Commission that because the northwest face of Châtillon was wired and the northeast face was not, the decision to shift a force of the 167th into the 168th's sector on the northeastern side was obvious, presumably so obvious that it did not need an author.

The remarkable part of General MacArthur's failure to lead during the action for Châtillon was that on the last day, October 16, he was absent from the movements of his two regiments. Actually, by forbidding the regiments to move together, objecting to the mixing of the regiments, he may have delayed the mixing that eventually was required. He failed to see that neither regiment could, in itself, put a sufficient force into Châtillon. In the matter of decisions there were some close places in the moves of the regiments when the action might have gone the other way, and while it could be argued that it was better to let the local commanders handle decisions, the decisions came at spots where an overall commander might well have been present. Notable examples were when the Germans at the top of Châtillon were massing for a counterattack around 3:00 p.m. and on the side of the 167th Sergeant Atkinson appeared on the scene with his mortar, while on the side of the 168th Captain Haynes at the request of Major Ross threw in his last two companies of the Second Battalion. At this time, when Haynes and his fellow officer had come into Ross's P.C. and spoken of the close situation on the front line, the moment could have taken the presence of someone with command of all the artillery supporting the Eighty-fourth Brigade, instead of the chance presence of an artillery officer at Major Ross's P.C. who said, "Let me fix it."

Last is the question of General MacArthur's immodesty, his willingness to take credit. The credit was almost presented to him. The commanding generals—Pershing, Summerall, and Menoher—all needed Châtillon. The commander in chief had seen his first two attacks in the Meuse-Argonne fail. The third, begun on October 14, was failing as well. The center of the third attack was to be a pincer with the Forty-second Division on one side and the Fifth on the other. Both divisions were to pass through the Kriemhilde Stellung and take the two villages on the Forty-second's side as well as Châtillon, and then take Côte Dame Marie, which had stood in the way of the Thirty-second Division. Instead the Forty-second stalled, and the Thirty-second took Dame Marie on its own unexpectedly. The Fifth failed so badly that its corps commander, Major General John L. Hines, relieved the division commander, a Pershing classmate, Major General John E. McMahon. Leaving aside the importance of Côte Dame Marie, south of the general AEF line and hence not as spectacular a capture as Châtillon to the north, the capture of the Côte de Châtillon was the single event that appeared as a victorious occasion. General Pershing needed Châtillon at a time when there was inter-Allied talk about reducing his responsibilities and shifting some of his divisions to French or British command, effectively reducing the AEF and whenever the eventual victory came reducing the role of President Wilson at the peace conference. In short, given the need for Châtillon, its capture gave a glow to any commander involved. All of which General MacArthur accepted as his due.

Perhaps it would have been too much, and yet one does not think so, to have expected him to seize every opportunity afterward to deflect the praise that came his way. Such behavior is not the usual course. There is a possibility that General MacArthur believed that he had led the troops. On the first day he observed from the brigade advanced P.C., a mile behind the line. During most of the three days, October 14–16, he was at his P.C. near Exermont, three miles from the fighting. From either place, all he could actually do was follow the reports of brigade observers at the P.C.'s of Major Ross and Lieutenant Colonel Bare.

Appendix

★ ★ ★ ★ ★ ★ ★ ★ ★ ★ ★ ★ ★ ★ ★ ★ ★ ★ ★ ★

Before and after American participation in the World War, General MacArthur was recommended for the Congressional Medal of Honor. Before 1917 the nomination may not have been important, for the medal had a checkered history. It might be said that it was the equivalent of the French Croix de Guerre, which French generals in 1914–1918 distributed with profligacy. In the Civil War the Congressional Medal possessed little value. In the Spanish-American War in 1898 its award did not mean much more. Major General William M. Wright, commander of the Eighty-ninth Division in 1918, testified that when he was an officer in Cuba he found himself conducted from one hill to another, during a maneuver in which no shots were fired, by a colonel who asked the officer in charge of the contingent to nominate him for the Congressional Medal. During the occupation of Veracruz in 1914 the U.S. Navy awarded forty-seven medals and the Marine Corps nine, for an operation that could not have seen much heroism. Major General Frederick Funston had gone in with a reinforced brigade, and the War Department considered replacing his men with a force commanded by General Leonard Wood and possibly sending Wood's force on to Mexico City to replace the then Mexican government. The rainy season had set in, and that meant sending Wood's force by rail. Funston had plenty of cars in Veracruz but few engines. Sent down from Washington as a member of Wood's staff, Captain MacArthur learned from a drunken Mexican engineer that there were engines at a nearby town, Alvarado, albeit outside Funston's lines. Bribing the engineer with $150 in gold, and enlisting two more Mexican assistants, who were unarmed, MacArthur set out on a reconnaissance, the group in a handcar. At Alvarado they found three engines, which MacArthur reported to the War Department as suitable but needing a few minor parts. In the course of going to and returning from Alvarado, Captain MacArthur shot seven hostile Mexicans—all bandits, not soldiers. The captain received three bullet holes through his clothes; one bullet passed through his shirt, and two struck the handcar within six inches of him. For this he was nominated for the Congressional Medal. The nomination was turned down by a War Department committee. The captain protested, and the committee confirmed the refusal.[1]

After the armistice in 1918 the then commander of the Forty-second Division, Major General C. A. F. Flagler, recommended General MacArthur for the medal, "For most distinguished gallantry in action northeast of Verdun on October 14, 1918." Although suffering from gas poisoning incurred less than thirty-six hours before, Flagler wrote, MacArthur voluntarily and with distinguished self-sacrifice left his sickbed to lead the attack of his brigade on Hills 288 and 242 and the Côte de Châtillon, the last the key to the entire German line. He sought to encourage his men so that

> in the prolonged, hand to hand and violent engagement that was under way, he might encourage and more effectively lead and guide the three engaged battalions, from the two regiments of his brigade, and afford them all available support from the means at his disposal. . . . General MacArthur put himself at the head of his men and took command of the line, in so doing and while exercising actual personal command in the field, he, at the same time, ensured and maintained communications both with the higher command and with the supporting and ancillary arms assigned to assist his brigade.

The recommendation was supported by two first lieutenants. One was Reginald H. Weller from the Eighty-fourth Infantry Brigade headquarters, a liaison officer throughout the period of the operations of the Forty-second Division northwest of Verdun. He said that General MacArthur, although on October 14 very weak, undergoing spells of vomiting, pushed forward afoot to the line and placed himself at the head of his brigade.

In so doing, he incurred the greatest peril and placed his life in immediate and constant danger. He made his way through a heavy interdic-
tion fire of gas and shrapnel and despite the machine gun fire and
artillery shelling of great intensity, executed with direct observation and
at close range on his lines, he joined his troops and took command of
the line. . . . He alone made victory possible. . . . the courage of General
MacArthur was the outstanding feature of the battle.

Lieutenant Wayne Hill, signal corps, attached to the headquarters of the
Eighty-fourth Brigade, was communications officer during the operations of
the Forty-second Division northwest of Verdun. He certified that Lieutenant
Weller was correct in all particulars of his certificate. Hill said that in his presence General Summerall told General MacArthur that Marshal Foch and
General Pershing had themselves that day told him those positions had to be
taken. General Summerall said that as commander of the First Division he
had tried to take the côte, and that General MacArthur must do so "at all
events." General MacArthur had four trunk lines back to higher headquarters. The lines were constantly broken because of intense artillery fire, and
they were difficult to repair because of gas laid down in the wooded valleys.
Nonetheless, the general is reported to have kept headquarters fully informed
and advised.[2]

Notes

★ ★

PREFACE

1. "Dined with [Major General Frank T.] Menoher and staff. After dinner, went to the 'P.C.' [post of command] of Brigadier General Douglas MacArthur beyond Exermont . . . an interesting talk . . . believes his 84th Infantry Brigade has done enough; that the 42nd Division has been pushed into critical situations too much, and that it is only a question of time when all the veteran soldiers will have been killed. MacArthur says it is difficult to get soldiers to go into severe fighting without being personally led by officers; that he himself had to lead his brigade 'through the wire' in recent fighting" (Rhodes diary, October 27, 1918).

"In my talk yesterday with General MacArthur, one thing impressed me particularly: the *scarcity of fighting commanders* as compared with the presence of *mere administrative officers*. And that many excellent fighting field officers become mere administrators when they reach general's rank! The time comes in every division, said MacArthur, when brigade or division commanders must instill 'the fighting spirit' into their commands *by personal presence and example*'" (emphasis in original; ibid., October 28).

2. Robert H. Ferrell, *America's Deadliest Battle: Meuse-Argonne, 1918.*

3. Henry J. Reilly, *Americans All: The Rainbow at War.*

4. James, *The Years of MacArthur,* 1:219–22. The biographer wrote, with evident error, "Upon hanging up the receiver, MacArthur calmly resumed his meeting, the group finally agreeing to try to sneak Ross's battalion around the hill to attack the Germans from the rear, with a massive frontal assault to follow immediately."

ONE. PREPARATION

1. By far the best account of 1917–1918 is Edward M. Coffman, *The War to End All Wars: The American Military Experience in World War I.*

2. Ibid., 11–17; Daniel R. Beaver, *Modernizing the American War Department: Change and Continuity in a Turbulent Era, 1885–1920;* Edward M. Coffman, *The Hilt of the Sword: The Career of Peyton C. March.*

3. For Pershing the classic accounts are two by Donald Smythe, *Guerrilla Warrior: The Early Life of John J. Pershing* and *Pershing: General of the Armies,* and Frank E. Vandiver, *Black Jack: The Life and Times of John J. Pershing.*

4. See the prescient articles by James W. Rainey, "Ambivalent Warfare: The Tactical Doctrine of the AEF in World War I" and "The Questionable Training of the AEF in World War I."

5. Allan Millett, "Over Where? The AEF and the American Strategy for Victory, 1917–1918."

6. Mark Ethan Grotelueschen has made notable strides in studying the change of tactics in the AEF, first in *Doctrine under Trial: American Artillery Employment in World War I,* then in a study of five divisions (the initial four together with the Seventy-seventh), *The AEF Way of War: The American Army and Combat in World War I.*

7. Timothy K. Nenninger, *The Leavenworth Schools and the Old Army: Education, Professionalism, and the Corps of the United States Army, 1881–1918.*

8. Ralph H. Van Deman, *The Final Memoranda: Major General Ralph H. Van Deman, USA Ret., 1865–1952, Father of U.S. Military Intelligence;* George B. Duncan, "Reminiscences of the World War," courtesy of Edward M. Coffman.

9. Robert H. Ferrell, *Collapse at Meuse-Argonne: The Failure of the Missouri-Kansas Division.*

10. James J. Cooke, *The Rainbow Division in the Great War.*

11. John W. Barry, *The Midwest Goes to War: The 32nd Division in the Great War.*

12. Evaluation of July 1, 1922, Pershing papers, box 23, Record Group 200, National Archives. Other commanders appraised him as excellent (Liggett), looks excellent (Bullard), very good but better as a staff officer, with a desire to please that makes him weak, reasonably aggressive, and needing more drive (Summerall).

13. It admittedly is difficult to estimate the qualities of many Regular officers, for they left few indications; they were by and large not inclined to self-appraisal. General Lenihan dictated his memories into a tape recorder, years later, and his wife, Mina, wrote his biography, "I Remember—I Remember." The memoir says nothing about the general's relief by General Summerall on October 15. For the latter see "Relief of Brigadier General Michael J. Lenihan," Pershing papers, entry 22, RG 200

(all citations followed by record group numbers are to the National Archives, College Park, Md.). Reilly, *Americans All*, 648–49.

14. Lloyd D. Ross, "History of Company M. Militia and National Guard, from October 18, 1893 to July 1, 1940," Iowa Historical Library, Des Moines. Courtesy of J. Garry Clifford.

15. Raymond Turner to the American Battle Monuments Commission, April 3, 1929, box 233, Forty-second Division, ABMC file, RG 117.

16. "As soon as we were around in the morning orders came to reconnoiter the ground one kilometer to our right and to move as soon as it was completed. This move was to relieve a part of the front of the Thirty-second Division and also to widen our sector. This move places my battalion directly in front of a high steep hill which we are going to have to attack. While reconnoitering our position we came in contact with the Boche and Sergeant Fleming and another of the scouts were captured. These are the first prisoners captured from this battalion. We made relief at 1:00 p.m. and established battalion headquarters in a deep freak hole with a foxhole halfway up the side of it for a nest for myself. The Boche from hill 286 however are enfilading my lines and occasionally put bursts of machine gun fire right into one side of the hole we are using for headquarters and his artillery is pounding all the time. Have just received a telephone that we are to attack in the morning. Orders later. It is raining again now but my shelter half keeps it out of my fox shelter" (Ross diary, Sunday, October 13, 1918).

TWO. OCTOBER 14

1. The Grady McWhiney Institute and the McWhiney Research Foundation carry on this scholarly work.

2. Francis P. Duffy, *Father Duffy's Story: A Tale of Humor and Heroism, of Life and Death with the Fighting Sixty-ninth*, 263. Duffy was a figure in New York City, and his statue is the only one of a priest erected in Manhattan (in Times Square). An excellent writer, he described his ambivalent nature to his friend Colonel Frank R. McCoy; he was a true warrior-priest: "You used to say you did not want any of yours not to enjoy this war. I certainly enjoyed it, and there was never a moment when I wanted to be any place else. And most particularly while you were with us [before promotion to brigadier general and assignment to the Thirty-second Division, McCoy was colonel of the 165th New York]. All parts of me were alive in that period—the old cloistered half of me that loved art and books and historical associations and artistic semi-tones in life and conversation, and the liberated swashbuckling personality that had had to pursue its adventures in daydreams by the monastery wall" (Duffy to McCoy, Thanksgiving Day 1918, McCoy papers).

3. Letter from R. B. DeLacour, November 16, 1926, box 232, Forty-second Division, ABMC file, RG 117.

4. Letter from Donovan in Reilly, *Americans All*, 692.

5. Martin J. Hogan, *The Shamrock Battalion in the Great War*, 243–47.

6. Letter from Bootz, April 5, 1930, box 232, Forty-second Division, ABMC file, RG 117.

7. Robert H. Ferrell, ed., *A Soldier in World War I: The Diary of Elmer W. Sherwood*. A forceful noncom in the heavy artillery regiment, Sherwood, like his fellows, hardly realized the straits of the 165th Infantry.

8. George E. Leach, *War Diary*, 56–57.

9. Albert M. Ettinger and A. Churchill Ettinger, *A Doughboy with the Fighting Sixty-ninth: A Remembrance of World War I*, 161.

10. Frederick Palmer, *Our Greatest Battle (the Meuse-Argonne)*, 88; letter from Johnson in Reilly, *Americans All*, 724.

11. See Chapter Three, 37–38.

12. *Our Greatest Battle*, 88; Summerall reported to General Liggett that Duffy was a disloyal member of the 165th, for which see the diary of Pierpont L. Stackpole, Liggett's aide. *Father Duffy's Story*, 272. *42nd Division, Summary of Operations in the World War*, contains casualty figures.

13. Beaumont B. Buck, *Memories of Peace and War*, 218–25.

14. *42nd Division, Summary of Operations in the World War*, 91.

15. R. M. Cheseldine, *Ohio in the Rainbow: Official Story of the 166th Infantry, 42nd Division, in the World War*, 244–45.

16. See Chapter Three, 42–43.

17. John H. Taber, *The Story of the 168th Infantry*, 2:167.

18. Letter from Witherell, October 8, 1926, box 233, Forty-second Division, ABMC file, RG 117.

19. The following is based on Ross's account in a letter in Reilly, *Americans All*, 668–73.

20. Field message, Forty-second Division historical, box 11, entry 1241, RG 120. Division records are notably lacking in after-action reports, but there are dozens of field messages, what appears to be a full set. They are approximately in order by the day and hour. The messages quoted subsequently are from the same source.

21. Rexmond C. Cochrane made admirable studies of German and AEF use of gas during 1917–1918, and one of the members of his small staff reviewed the accumulation of German documents; see Cochrane, *The 42nd Division before Landres-et-St. Georges*, 46n.

22. Letter from Wells, November 23, Forty-second Division, box 233, ABMC file, RG 117; letter from Bare in Reilly, *Americans All*, 677–78.

23. Field messages, Forty-second Division historical, box 11, entry 1241, RG 120.

THREE. OCTOBER 15

1. Letter from Donovan in Reilly, *Americans All*, 695–97.

2. For what follows see "Relief of Brigadier General Michael J. Lenihan," Pershing papers, box 8, entry 22, RG 200; *Father Duffy's Story*, 266–67.

3. Duffy wrote his friend Colonel McCoy on Thanksgiving Day, 1918, when censorship had ended with the armistice, that one could not send riflemen to attack untouched wire and trenches defended by machine guns and artillery; he said that Summerall was "mad as the devil" and known as von Summerall (McCoy papers).

4. *42nd Division: Summary of Operations in the World War*, 91.

5. Cheseldine, *Ohio in the Rainbow*, 25.

6. Ibid., 256. The colonel's aide was Robert Beightler, his adjutant, who became commanding general of Ohio's Thirty-seventh Division in World War II; Beightler was one of two National Guard generals to survive in command after nationalization of the Guard in 1940. In the earlier war he was privy to Hough's thinking on all matters pertaining to the 166th Regiment and ever afterward maintained that AEF army, corps, and division generals, Regulars, wasted the lives of their men in futile attacks against impregnable positions. See the excellent biography by John Kennedy Ohl, *Minuteman: The Military Career of General Robert S. Beightler:* "To Beightler, what he saw at the Kriemhildestellung was not the way to conduct a battle or to lead men" (36).

7. For the 168th Iowa the best source is Taber, *Story of the 168th Infantry*. It needs comparison with the ABMC file, RG 117; *42nd Division: Summary of Operations in the World War;* and Major Ross's diary.

8. Taber, *Story of the 168th Infantry*, 2:168.

9. Letter from Ross in Reilly, *Americans All*, 172.

10. Field messages, Forty-second Division historical, box 11, entry 1241, RG 120.

11. Letter from Witherell, October 8, 1926, box 233, Forty-second Division, ABMC file, RG 117; Taber, *Story of the 168th Infantry*, 2:185.

12. Letter from Screws in Reilly, *Americans All*, 345–46.

13. Letter from Bare in ibid., 348–50.

14. Letter from MacArthur in ibid., 317–18.

15. W. Kerr Rainsford, *From Upton to the Meuse: With the Three Hundred and Seventh Infantry*, xviii–xx. This book almost certainly came to the attention of General MacArthur.

16. Letter from Bare in Reilly, *Americans All*, 348–50.

17. McCoy to Duffy (McCoy papers).

18. Field messages, Forty-second Division historical, box 11, entry 1241, RG 120.

19. Letter from Ross in Reilly, *Americans All*, 672. "After dark General MacArthur orders us to proceed to the Côte de Châtillon by using the bayonet, but on account

of the wire and brush it is absolutely impossible and as I was reluctant to try it he later withdrew the order" (Ross diary, Monday, October 14, 1918).

20. Letter from Little, November 26, 1926, Forty-second Division, box 233, ABMC file, RG 117.

21. Letter from Norris in Reilly, *Americans All,* 680–81.

22. Letter from Bare in ibid., 678–79.

23. Letter from Hughes in ibid., 659.

24. Letter from Winn in ibid., 711–12.

FOUR. OCTOBER 16

1. Letter from Winn in Reilly, *Americans All,* 712–13.

2. The colonel was Babcock, formerly of the First Division, relieved by Summerall. See William M. Wright, *Meuse-Argonne Diary: A Division Commander in World War I,* 135–36.

3. Letter from Witherell, October 8, 1926, box 233, Forty-second Division, ABMC file, RG 117.

4. Taber, *Story of the 168th Infantry,* 2:191–92.

5. Letter from Ross, December 2, 1926, box 233, Forty-second Division, ABMC file, RG 117.

6. Taber, *Story of the 168th Infantry,* 2:194.

7. Letter from Little, November 26, 1926, box 233, Forty-second Division, ABMC file, RG 117.

8. Letter from Major Norris in Reilly, *Americans All,* 684–86.

9. Field messages, Forty-second Division historical, box 11, entry 1241, RG 120.

10. Letter from Atkinson in Reilly, *Americans All,* 687.

11. Cooke, *Rainbow Division in the Great War,* 179.

12. Field messages, Forty-second Division historical, box 11, entry 1241, RG 120.

13. *42nd Division: Summary of Operations in the World War,* 91. In the 168th Iowa Regiment, Major Ross took the most casualties in his First Battalion: "My battalion is sure shot to pieces. We had a strength in the infantry when we entered on the engagements of 849. In three days we lost fifteen officers wounded, forty-four enlisted men killed, and 295 enlisted men wounded, thirty-seven missing and fifty-seven sick and exhausted from exposure, machine gun [company] seven killed, twenty-seven wounded, three officers sick, and ten men sick from exposure. Strength machine gun company today two officers and 134 men. Strength infantry companies today seven officers, 425 men. Companies organized as two platoons and short of sergeants to lead them" (Ross diary, October 21, 1918).

14. Letter from Ravee Norris in Reilly, *Americans All,* 685–86.

15. Stewart, *Rainbow Bright,* 124–25.

16. Taber, *Story of the 168th Infantry,* 2:202.

17. See divisional and other gas studies by Rexmond C. Cochrane, notably *42nd Division before Landres-et-St. Georges.*

18. Intelligence summaries, box 17, Forty-second Division historical, entry 1231, RG 120.

19. Amerine, *Alabama's Own in France,* 11–12.

FIVE. CONCLUSION

1. "The Relief and Reduction of Brigadier General R. A. Brown, 84th Brigade," Pershing papers, RG 200. The then Captain Ross had been assigned to the First Battalion but was not yet its commander. Brown's relief disgusted him. "General Brown has been relieved and ordered to the states and General MacArthur becomes our brigadier. We have all been expecting it but feel sorry for General Brown and ourselves as well. I sure want to keep out of his [MacArthur's] sight so he won't want to keep me here and assign me to some other command. I want to go home now that they have fooled me so much and for so long. Lt. Wright has been detached and the general's aide so I become captain of operations and intelligence" (Ross diary, August 5, 1918).

2. The Babcock memoir, a huge typescript, is in the Hoover Institution at Palo Alto, Calif.

APPENDIX

1. James, *Years of MacArthur,* 1:115–27. In 1916, Congress asked for a review of the 2,625 medals issued. A committee of five retired generals chaired by Lieutenant General Nelson Miles, himself a medal winner, rescinded 911 medals and required the winners then living to return their rescinded medals. A result of the committee's work was creation of a "pyramid of honor" establishing the hierarchy of medals.

2. Courtesy MacArthur Foundation, Norfolk, Virginia.

Sources

★ ★

As remarked in the Preface, the division history by General Henry J. Reilly, although a large piece of evidence, was also the most frustrating one. It required careful reading and then, because of Reilly's essential inability to organize, an equally careful rearranging. I found that I needed to take the testimonies he acquired between 1931 and the publication in 1936 of his massive, unindexed book, all 888 pages, and rearrange them by the three days of the action. Reilly's own commentaries were of uncertain usefulness, for he was given to incautious analysis, comments that were more resounding than careful. In addition, the general made numerous errors in spelling, for example changing Bare to Baer and Fallaw to Fallow. One must also wonder about the accuracy of the punctuation in his quotations and about what a very careful scholar—the student of gas warfare in 1917–1918, Rexmond C. Cochrane—believed to have been changes in wording that might have shifted the points being made by the letter writers of 1931–1936. These changes General Reilly buried in the 130 boxes of unorganized papers, about which I learned from my friend Richard J. Sommers, that Reilly sent to the U.S. Army Military History Institute at Carlisle Barracks in Pennsylvania.

Other than mining, so to speak, General Reilly's divisional history and papers, the most obvious sources were the letters solicited by the American Battle Monuments Commission from former members of the AEF in 1926–1930 or thereabouts. After officers of the ABMC in Washington, under guidance of the commission's chairman, General Pershing, discovered addresses and sent out letters of solicitation, and received answers, they annotated them, comparing each letter with such others as were on hand. They changed their maps accordingly, often after stamping parts of a letter as "accepted" and others as "not accepted." The descriptions of the actions, in the present case the attacks of the Forty-second Division between October 14 and 16, they combined into narratives. During World War II, for the most part in 1944, the ABMC published its battle narratives for 1917–1918 in a series of booklets, one for each active division in the AEF, twenty-nine booklets in all. Each booklet has a sleeve of large-scale maps. Just after World War II, the army brought out *United States Army in the World War* (Washington, D.C.: Government Printing Office, 1948), compiling in seventeen volumes what seemed the most important documents relating to American participation in the earlier war. I have not found these documents of much use, as they tend to be field orders (which the present book has found to be superficial, not followed by units in the field, as in the cases of the four regiments of the Forty-second). They have value as an immediate source but require much further investigation.

In the National Archives in College Park, Maryland, the divisional files usually are the first place of resort. The Division files in the archives are wonderfully detailed, such as those of the Seventy-seventh Division during its troubles in early October in attempting to relieve the five hundred men of the Lost Battalion (which had companies from two battalions and never was lost). The attempts of the brigade commander, General Evan M. Johnson, to reach the men, and his frustrating relations with his division commander, Major General Robert Alexander, who believed that the way to prompt General Johnson into action was to insult him, are much in evidence. For the Seventy-seventh Division there are frank after-action reports by unit commanders below the brigade and regimental levels. The same holds for other divisions, notably the Thirty-fifth, which failed during the first attack of the AEF in the Meuse-Argonne, September 26–October 1. The failure also appears in an eighty-one-page, single-spaced, legal-size, typewritten report by the inspector general of I Corps, Lieutenant Colonel Robert G. Peck (only a summary copy of which is in the Thirty-fifth Division file, the entire report being in the papers of Brigadier General Hugh A. Drum at the U.S. Army Military History Institute in Carlisle Barracks).

Unfortunately, however, the divisional files of the Forty-Second are poor. The division did not keep good files. Cochrane remarked it when bringing out his study on the division, and it is obvious to any student who searches through them.

One might have hoped for the personal papers of general officers of the Forty-second Division to have been deposited by those officers at Carlisle Barracks. There are none. General Summerall's papers are in the manuscript division of the Library of Congress but are sketchy and filled with choleric comments about General Pershing's memoirs, the publication of which annoyed Summerall (especially in regard to his part in the so-called race to Sedan inspired by Pershing in the last days of the war). General Frank T. Menoher left nothing, save his praise of General MacArthur in the *New York Times* after the armistice, a copy of a recommendation for the Distinguished Service Cross. General Michael J. Lenihan's widow gave her account of her husband's career to the Military History Institute but omitted the events of October 14–15, whether at the general's suggestion or on her own. General MacArthur took his personal papers to the Philippines in 1935, and in 1942 the Japanese captured them. In the virtual sack of Manila in 1945, when a Japanese rear admiral marshaled the troops in the city and defended Manila block by block, the papers disappeared.

General MacArthur's personal file as an army officer, known as his 201 file, is now open at the federal records center in St. Louis.

Major General Rhodes, to whom General MacArthur spoke about Châtillon during the last days of the war, gave a copy of his diary to the archives at Carlisle Barracks. Another is in the National Archives.

The papers of the commanders of the 167th and 168th regiments for the Côte de Châtillon vary widely in quality. Both Lieutenant Colonel Walter E. Bare and Major Lloyd D. Ross were first-rate commanders. The Bare papers, still unorganized, are in the Alabama Department of Archives and History in Montgomery. They consist of a single box, and for the military actions of 1918 the colonel left only division field messages, which for Châtillon proved of little value. The papers of Major Ross are something else, principally a huge diary for his service in 1917–1919, until the division took ship on the *Leviathan* back to the United States. In addition, he saved his field orders. In 1940, when he retired from the Iowa National Guard, there was a collection of testimony from former associates, and General MacArthur wrote from

Manila; a copy of the retirement proceedings is in Ross's papers. As mentioned in the Acknowledgments, the papers are in possession of his granddaughter Martha Braley in Des Moines.

Amerine, William H. *Alabama's Own in France.* New York: Eaton and Gettinger, 1919.

Anon. *Iodine and Gasoline: A History of the 117th Sanitary Train.* N.p.: n.d.

Barbee, David Rankin. "The D'Artagnon of the Army." *Washington Post,* October 26, 1930.

Bare, Walter E. Papers. Alabama Department of Archives and History, Montgomery.

Barry, John W. *The Midwest Goes to War: The 32nd Division in the Great War.* Lanham, Md.: Scarecrow, 2007.

Bauer, Richard E. *The Spirit of the Guard: The Iowa National Guard in Two World Wars.* Lake Mills, Iowa: Graphic, 1981.

Beaver, Daniel R. *Modernizing the American War Department: Change and Continuity in a Turbulent Era, 1885–1920.* Kent: Kent State University Press, 2006.

Bishop, Jim and Virginia. *Fighting Father Duffy.* New York: Vision, 1956.

Brown, Warren J. *Child Yank over the Rainbow Division, 1918.* Largo, Fla.: Aero-Medical, 1977.

Buck, Beaumont B. *Memories of Peace and War.* San Antonio, Tex.: Naylor, 1935.

Cheseldine, R. M. *Ohio in the Rainbow: Official Story of the 166th Infantry, 42nd Division, in the World War.* Columbus: Heer, 1924.

Cochrane, Rexmond C. *The 42nd Division before Landres-et-St. Georges, October 1918.* Washington, D.C.: U.S. Army Chemical Corps, 1959.

Coffman, Edward M. *The Hilt of the Sword: The Career of Peyton C. March.* Madison: University of Wisconsin Press, 1966.

———. *The Old Army: A Portrait of the American Army in Peacetime, 1784–1898.* New York: Oxford University Press, 1986.

———. *The Regulars: The Army Officer, 1898–1941.* Cambridge: Harvard University Press, 2004.

———. *The War to End All Wars: The American Military Experience in World War I.* New York: Oxford University Press, 1968.

Collins, Louis L. *History of the 151st Field Artillery, Rainbow Division.* St. Paul: Minnesota War Commission, 1924.

Congressional Medal of Honor, the Distinguished Service Cross, and the Distinguished Service Medal. Washington, D.C.: Government Printing Office, 1920.

Cooke, James J. *Pershing and His Generals: Command and Staff in the AEF.* Westport, Conn.: Praeger, 1997.

———. *The Rainbow Division in the Great War.* Westport, Conn.: Praeger, 1994.

DeWeerd, Harvey A. *President Wilson Fights the War: World War I and the American Intervention.* New York: Macmillan, 1968.

Donovan, William J. Papers. U.S. Army Military History Institute, Carlisle Barracks, Pa.

Duffy, Francis P. *Father Duffy's Story: A Tale of Humor and Heroism, of Life and Death with the Fighting Sixty-ninth.* New York: Doran, 1919.

Eisenhower, John S. D. *Yanks: The Epic Story of the American Army in World War I.* New York: Free Press, 2001.

Ettinger, Albert M., and A. Churchill Ettinger. *A Doughboy with the Fighting Sixty-ninth: A Remembrance of World War I.* Shippensburg, Pa.: White Mane, 1992.

Ferrell, Robert H. *America's Deadliest Battle: Meuse-Argonne, 1918.* Lawrence: University Press of Kansas, 2007.

———. *Collapse at Meuse-Argonne: The Failure of the Missouri-Kansas Division.* Columbia: University of Missouri Press, 2004.

———, ed. *A Soldier in World War I: The Diary of Elmer W. Sherwood.* Indianapolis: Indiana Historical Society Press, 2004.

42nd Division: Summary of Operations in the World War. Washington, D.C.: Government Printing Office, 1944.

Frank, Richard B. *MacArthur.* New York: Palgrave Macmillan, 2007.

Grotelueschen, Mark Ethan. *The AEF Way of War: The American Army and Combat in World War I.* New York: Cambridge University Press, 2007.

———. *Doctrine under Trial: American Artillery Employment in World War I.* Westport, Conn.: Greenwood, 2001.

Harris, Stephen L. *Duffy's War: Fr. Francis Duffy, Wild Bill Donovan, and the Irish Fighting 69th in World War I.* Washington, D.C.: Potomac, 2006.

Hogan, Martin J. *The Shamrock Battalion of the Rainbow: A Story of the "Fighting Sixty Ninth."* Edited by James J. Cooke. Columbia: University of Missouri Press, 2007.

Huber, Richard M. *Big All the Way Through: The Life of Van Santvoord Merle-Smith.* Princeton: Princeton University Class of 1911, 1951.

Hurley, Alfred. *Billy Mitchell: Crusader for Air Power.* Bloomington: Indiana University Press, 1975.

James, D. Clayton. *The Years of MacArthur.* 3 vols. Boston: Houghton Mifflin, 1970–1985.

Langille, Leslie. *Men of the Rainbow.* Chicago: O'Sullivan, 1933.

Leach, George E. *War Diary.* Roanoke, Va.: Rainbow Division Veterans, 1962.

Lenihan, Michael J. "I Remember—I Remember." Told to Mina W. Lenihan, ca. 1956–1957. U.S. Army Military History Institute, Carlisle Barracks, Pa.

MacArthur, Charles. *War Bugs.* Garden City, N.Y.: Doubleday, Doran, 1929.

MacArthur, Douglas. *Reminiscences.* New York: McGraw-Hill, 1964.

McCoy, Frank R. Papers. Library of Congress, Washington, D.C.

Menoher, Frank T. "Pays High Tribute to Gen. MacArthur." *New York Times,* December 28, 1918.

Millett, Allan. "Over Where? The AEF and the American Strategy for Victory, 1917–1918." In Kenneth J. Hagan and William R. Roberts, eds., *Against All Enemies: Interpretations of American Military History from Colonial Times to the Present.* Westport, Conn.: Greenwood, 1986.

Minnegerode, F. L. "General MacArthur Rises to the Top." *New York Times,* August 17, 1930.

Nenninger, Timothy K. "John J. Pershing and Relief for Cause in the American Expeditionary Forces, 1917–1918." *Army History* (2005): 21–32.

———. *The Leavenworth Schools and the Old Army: Education, Professionalism, and the Corps of the United States Army, 1881–1918.* Westport, Conn.: Greenwood, 1978.

———. "Tactical Dysfunction in the AEF: 1917–1918." *Military Affairs* 51 (1987): 177–81.

———. "Unsystematic as a Mode of Command: Commanders and the Process of Command in the American Expeditionary Forces, 1917–1918." *Journal of Military History* 64 (2000): 739–68.

Ohl, John Kennedy. *Minuteman: The Military Career of General Robert S. Beightler.* Boulder, Colo.: Rienner, 2001.

150th Field Artillery United States, in Memory of the Indianapolis Rainbow. Veterans Association of Marion County, Indiana, 1927.

Palmer, Frederick. *Our Greatest Battle (the Meuse-Argonne).* New York: Dodd, Mead, 1919.

Palmerton, Paul L., ed. *Under the Rainbow: Battery F, 150th F.A.: A History of its Services in the War against Germany.* Indianapolis: Battery F, 1919.

Pershing, John J. *My Experiences in the World War.* 2 vols. New York: Stokes, 1931.

Rainey, James W. "Ambivalent Warfare: The Tactical Doctrine of the AEF in World War I." *Parameters* 13 (1983): 34–45.

———. "The Questionable Training of the AEF in World War I." *Parameters* 22 (1992–1993): 89–103.

Rainsford, W. Kerr. *From Upton to the Meuse: With the Three Hundred and Seventh Infantry.* New York: Appleton, 1920.

Reilly, Henry J. *Americans All: The Rainbow at War.* Columbus: Heer, 1936.

———. Papers. U.S. Army Military History Institute, Carlisle Barracks, Pa.

Report of the Secretary of War to the President: 1926. Washington, D.C.: Government Printing Office, 1926.

Rhodes, Charles D. Diary. U.S. Army Military History Institute, Carlisle Barracks, Pa.

Robb, Winfred E. *The Price of Our Heritage.* Des Moines: American Lithograph and Printing, 1919.

Ross, Lloyd D. "History of Company 'M,' Militia and National Guard, from October 18, 1893 to July 1, 1940." Iowa Historical Library, Des Moines.

———. Papers. Possession of Martha Braley, Des Moines, Iowa.

Smythe, Donald J. *Guerrilla Warrior: The Early Life of John J. Pershing.* New York: Scribner, 1973.

———. *Pershing: General of the Armies.* Bloomington: Indiana University Press, 1988.

Stewart, Lawrence O. *Rainbow Bright.* Philadelphia: Dorrance, 1923.

Straub, Elmer Frank. *A Sergeant's Diary in the World War.* Indianapolis: Indiana Historical Bureau, 1923.

Summerall, Charles P. Papers. Library of Congress, Washington, D.C.

Taber, John H. *The Story of the 168th Infantry.* 2 vols. Iowa City: State Historical Society, 1925.

Thompson, Hugh S. *Trench Knives and Mustard Gas: With the 42nd Rainbow Division in France.* Edited by Robert H. Ferrell. College Station: Texas A&M University Press, 2004.

Tompkins, Raymond S. *The Story of the Rainbow Division.* New York: Boni and Liveright, 1919.

Van Deman, Ralph H. *The Final Memoranda: Major General Ralph H. Van Deman, USA Ret., 1865–1952, Father of U.S. Military Intelligence.* Edited by Ralph E. Weber. Wilmington, Del.: Scholarly Resources, 1988.

Vandiver, Frank E. *Black Jack: The Life and Times of John J. Pershing.* College Station: Texas A & M University Press, 1977.

Votaw, John F. *The American Expeditionary Forces in World War I.* Oxford, Eng.: Osprey, 2005.

Weigley, Russell F. *The American Way of War: A History of United States Military Strategy and Policy.* New York: Macmillan, 1973.

———. *History of the United States Army.* New York: Macmillan, 1967.

Wolf, Walter B. *A Brief History of the Rainbow Division.* New York: Rand McNally, 1919.

Wright, William M. *Meuse-Argonne Diary: A Division Commander in World War I.* Ed. Robert H. Ferrell. Columbia: University of Missouri Press, 2004.

Index

★ ★